High-
MAINTENANCE
Employees

Why Your Best People Will Also Be Your Most Difficult... and What You Can Do about It

Katherine Graham Leviss

 SOURCEBOOKS, INC.
NAPERVILLE, ILLINOIS

This publication is designed to provide accurate and authoritative information in regard to the subject matter covered. It is sold with the understanding that the publisher is not engaged in rendering legal, accounting, or other professional service. If legal advice or other expert assistance is required, the services of a competent professional person should be sought.—From a Declaration of Principles Jointly Adopted by a Committee of the American Bar Association and a Committee of Publishers and Associations

All brand names and product names used in this book are trademarks, registered trademarks, or trade names of their respective holders. Sourcebooks, Inc., is not associated with any product or vendor in this book.

Published by Sourcebooks, Inc.
P.O. Box 4410, Naperville, Illinois   60567-4410
(630) 961-3900
FAX: (630) 961-2168
www.sourcebooks.com

Library of Congress Cataloging-in-Publication Data
Graham Leviss, Katherine.
  High-maintenance employees : why your best people will also be your most difficult...and what you can do about it / Katherine Graham Leviss.
      p. cm.
  Includes index.
  ISBN-13: 978-1-4022-0623-8
  ISBN-10: 1-4022-0623-2
  1. Problem employees. 2. Problem employees--Counseling of. 3. Supervision of employees. 4. Employee motivation. 5. Personnel management. I. Title.

HF5549.5.E42G72 2005
658.3'045--dc22

                                                                                    2005025008

Printed and bound in the United States of America.
LB   10 9 8 7 6 5 4 3 2 1

DEDICATION

To my husband Evan for believing in me and supporting me through every new project, no matter how daunting; for graciously giving me and our son your love, time, and patience, and for your advice and encouragement; to my son Ethan for being the source of joy, perspective, and renewal when I needed it most.

CONTENTS

ACKNOWLEDGMENTS

Thank you to all of the XB clients, colleagues, and friends—too many to mention individually—who graciously gave your time, expertise, and caring.

To Patricia Fripp for ingeniously guiding me to the idea for this book and inspiring me to write it.

Special thanks to Carol Hanley for believing in me and supporting me through this and many other projects.

To Jim Mastors and Janet Pendexter for their partnership, commitment, and belief in XB; for your success using and validating many of the models in this book.

To Claudia Gere for her patient coaching and editing; for showing me how to publish this book—it would not have happened without her.

To Natalie Manor, the catalyst for starting this book, with her wonderful intuition for having the right big idea at the right time and for introducing me to Claudia.

To Annie McGuire for embracing my ideas, championing me and my work, and validating the concepts in this book.

To Tim Ursini for his guidance and coaching, for giving me courage to do the unimaginable, and for leading me to the publisher.

To Cindy Fox for her devotion, friendship, and patience; for shouldering the extra workload, which gave me the time and focus to write.

Jake Karger for her friendship, brilliant ideas, and amazing creativity.

To Susan Travers, my stalwart assistant, for forging ahead, with enthusiasm and dedication, on any task I threw her way.

To my dearest friends, my heart-felt gratitude: Barbara Rose for her sincere love and for as long as I can remember steadfastly cheering me on, and Tricia Baker, who showed me early in my career it's possible have a great boss as a friend.

To my wonderful parents, Karen and Jim Graham, for their love, influence, and support; for helping me become who I am.

How I Discovered I Was a High-Maintenance Employee and Developed a Winning Management Strategy

"Nature has given us two ears, two eyes, and but one tongue—to the end, we should hear and see more than we speak."
—Socrates

I first heard the term high maintenance when I was in high school. It was 1981. I was standing just outside a classroom, about to go in, when I heard a couple of my teachers talking. They didn't know I was there. I stopped when one mentioned my name.

"That Kathi is good, but she's definitely high maintenance. She's driving me crazy," the teacher said.

"I know what you mean; she can't hear the word 'no.' I'm exhausted just listening to her; I can't believe the energy she has."

Hearing these two teachers talk, I thought to myself, "They couldn't possibly be talking about me. They don't have any idea what they're talking about. I am not high maintenance... am I?"

I immediately knew what high maintenance meant, and I knew they weren't talking about my makeup and hairstyle. I remember feeling hurt and angry, and it was then I understood that, in their eyes, I was too demanding.

I learned very early in life that I was high maintenance. I knew my drive for success was so important that it didn't matter how much energy it took to achieve my goals, even if it exhausted those around me. As my life went on, I began to discover in my coworkers and others the following personality traits that I exhibited throughout my life.

High-Maintenance Employees Are Demanding

I don't think that there was ever a time in my life where I wouldn't be described as "demanding." But I just wanted to get things done. I was relentless in my pursuit of whatever goal I was chasing at the moment. I was president of my senior class and these teachers were my advisors. They were supposed to help our class fulfill its duties before graduation. When I thought something should be done or I had an idea about exactly how something should be done, I wouldn't let up. I was pushing them for approval on projects that were well beyond the scope any class before us had tackled. These teachers obviously thought I was wasting their time. But, in my eyes, I was getting the job done right so I could get on to something else, something bigger, and something even more exciting.

High-Maintenance Employees Do Not Operate as Team Players

My teachers also thought of me as not being a team player because I always had my own agenda. It was hard for me to hear about another approach or plan other than the one I had, especially if, in my view, it wasn't going to get the same level of results. I've come a long way since then in understanding how teams work. But early on, I didn't know what it really meant to be a team player. I liked being the leader so I could get things done.

High-Maintenance Employees Are Uncompromising

We were the only high-school class that had money allocated for reunion activities every five years up to the twenty-fifth year reunion. We'd come up with fundraising ideas and different creative ways to make that money. My teachers just saw me as high energy, but I saw myself as somebody who had high goals and knew how to achieve them. I saw myself as a high performer.

High-Maintenance Employees Are Driven

In my very first job out of college I learned that high energy has its limits. I was hired by a station in a top-ten radio market to sell advertising time. My first boss gave me a revenue goal each month. This was not motivating to me.

I remember thinking, "Don't show me the number. I'm doing everything I can possibly do and if you show me the number, it's just going to make me anxious. I will do whatever it takes and I will be successful. Don't limit me by giving me a goal. Let me know if you have a problem with my performance so I can fix it."

Knowing what the goals were, I had to exceed them at every measure because I was so self-motivated. The revenue goal was more of a distraction because I had my own goal in mind and I always overperformed.

I remember one time, however, when I disappointed my boss. I found there were periods of time when I would just have to decompress. I remember my father saying when I was young, "You can't keep up that energy level; you'll have to crash at some point."

I remember looking at him, feeling puzzled and saying, "You have no idea what you're talking about." Today, over twenty years later, I know that he knew exactly what he was talking about.

High-Maintenance Employees Behave Disrespectfully

With another employer in the radio industry, I learned a lesson in respect at a company meeting. While sitting in the meeting, I received a client request in my email. It was an informal meeting; in fact, some of us were sitting on the floor. As the president was conducting the meeting, I was typing a response to the client's request. I was listening, but I was also pursuing my own goal of getting something out to my client.

Later someone took me aside and told me how inappropriate my behavior was. She did it in a nice and tactful way. It never occurred to me that what I was doing was disrespectful to anyone. That's how focused I was on getting the job done and on my own agenda.

High-Maintenance Employees Can Be Intimidating

Several times in my career I have worked for managers who I felt were poor leaders. When I recognized these managers were incapable of managing up to my standards, I had very little interaction with them. I would try to work without them and around them. I did my best to avoid ever communicating with them. I knew, once I made contact, I'd have to explain everything I was doing. Naturally, I was viewed as uncooperative. I also think, because of my avoidance tactics, these bosses may have been too intimidated to approach me.

It was another lesson in respect. Looking back I could have handled that much differently… and much better. When I say differently, I mean I would have been a lot more respectful to them as people. I wasn't mean or nasty, but I avoided them because I didn't tolerate incompetence very well.

High-Maintenance Employees Are Emotional

I like to work fast, and to make decisions fast and from my gut. But one of the managers I had undid everything I did. For example, one day I fired someone in the department. She didn't have another job to go to, so I told her she could use our office for a few weeks until she found something else. One day I heard her talking on the phone about how messed up she thought the company was, so I told her she had to leave immediately. I didn't think it was fair for the rest of my team to have to put up with her negativity about our company. My boss went to her after I'd asked her to leave and told her she could continue to use the office.

Even though I still don't agree with my boss's decision to let someone who was badmouthing the company stick around, I've learned a lot since then about how I need to slow down my decision process and think through more carefully the consequences of my decisions. Though I still trust my gut instincts and would make the same decision today in that situation, I ask a lot more questions and surround myself with people that help me think things through from different perspectives.

High-Maintenance Employees Are Uncooperative

From radio, I moved into a career in the television industry. I worked in television for five years and I had several different bosses. I think the bosses who valued my work or understood how to empower me were probably very much like me in how they operated. And they saw that I could produce real results for them.

There were others that didn't quite know what to do with me. One boss would communicate with me by taking me out to breakfast. During breakfast he would say in a very demanding way, "Here's what you're gonna do. Here is the change you will make."

I immediately became defensive and uncooperative. I lost count of how many times I took out my résumé during the year I worked for that boss. The best approach for him to use with me would have been, "I'm thinking about some changes and I think your strengths would really complement our team and this is where we could use your talents. Let's talk about that. I have a couple of ideas."

I was not one to hide my feelings or my anger. It was very easy for me to lose my temper and get very emotional. Later I learned to control my temper and to talk only after I've had time to think about what I want to do and say.

High-Maintenance Employees Are Defiant

Right after I left my last job in television, I became a sales manager for another company. I had decided that I wanted to go back to school to get an MBA degree.

I had worked several years hiring and building a new staff for this company and then executing a new business model. My efforts had finally begun to pay off. Two weeks before the school year started, I received a call from the owner of the company. He said, "I have a great opportunity for you. I am partnering with a new company, and I would like you to run it. This will be your MBA program. You can learn everything you need to know about business there." He then proceeded to tell me that to secure the acquisition deal, he had agreed to give my job to the sales manager of the other company. I had no choice. I was to take the new position or be out of a job. I didn't have to think about my employer's offer. I was being told what to do without a choice. That evening, I began to clean out my office.

The next day I was told to make the announcement to my staff. This change meant that each of my staff had to apply for their jobs with this new sales manager and compete with his existing staff. No one from the senior management team even bothered to come to the meeting to address my staff. I was so disappointed with the lack of moral support from upper management, and even though it was probably what everyone in the room was thinking, I made the mistake of telling my staff how angry I was. I did not hide how I felt and I was not going to have my employer make any choices for me. Since then, I've learned how to keep my cool.

High-Maintenance Employees Are Erratic

I have held many positions from account executive to sales manager to vice president. After about my sixth job by age thirty, I began to wonder if I'd ever be fulfilled in a job. It wasn't until several years later that I realized what was going on. I loved my job when I was working on new projects or new problems. But once each project was completed, I found myself bored and unhappy until something fresh came along.

It was the thrill of something new that excited me and kept me going. When the thrill was gone, I wasn't quite sure what to do with myself.

If my managers had let me know that they had a new project in the works for me, I would have had something to look forward to...something to keep my mind (and my energy) occupied. It's sort of like when the wedding is over and you get post-wedding depression. Most high-maintenance employees are unhappy when a project is over and they don't have another one in sight.

It was my craving for new challenges and my constant desire to create innovative ideas and approaches that led me to the realization that I needed to run my own company.

High-Maintenance Employees Are Driven to Succeed

One company I worked for introduced me to the concept of behaviors and the different styles people have for communicating and doing their work. I answered a questionnaire that asked me to choose what word or phrase out of a group of four best described my preferences. My responses resulted in a behavioral profile that told me about my preferred operating style.

The first time I looked at the finished profile, I had an epiphany. My profile said something about always having the next project or new ideas to work on. After all those years, it finally hit me that I need to be the person who creates the new project or thinks up the new ideas. Once the new project is done, then I need to come up with another project.

The profile also pointed out what I need to be aware of to be successful. It stressed how important it is for me to work with process-oriented people who like to work each detail and who like implementation, process, and workflow. When I can hand off the detail work to someone who can help implement my ideas, I can move on to the next project more quickly.

The profile put key elements of my previous career experiences into perspective for me for the first time. Even as I rapidly climbed the corporate ladder, from account executive to sales manager to co-owner and managing director, I was never satisfied unless I had control over the results I was responsible for. I also needed to have new challenges and know they were waiting for me when I finished the current project.

Now, as president of my own company, after I create a new program and I feel it meets my quality standards, the process-oriented people I've hired continue to train on those new programs while I go off and create something new. I found the secret ingredient for keeping myself challenged. I also recognized the type of work environment that suits me best.

In the following chapters, I will take you through my experience as I transformed from an unruly racehorse to a thoroughbred winner and how you can win the corporate race by transforming yourself or by better managing the High-Maintenance High Performers (HMHP) on your team.

Every organization has high-maintenance employees: the leaders, the movers, the decision makers. High-maintenance employees are winners with all of the attributes for success when given the right training, guidance, and room to run. High-maintenance employees give companies breakthrough thinking, so important for today's changing and adapting businesses. *High-Maintenance Employees: Why Your Best People Will Also Be Your Most Difficult... and What You Can Do about It* will tell you how these people operate best and the secrets of managing them for the results you and your company need. This book contains the techniques that have taught thousands of front-line managers and employees. They in turn have used these techniques to create highly productive teams. New thinking and fast results are more crucial than ever; companies need people who set the pace.

This book examines the behavior style most often found in those people who are the leaders, innovators, overachievers, decision-makers, won't-quit results drivers, who are also most often responsible for businesses' successes. It wasn't until I took my first behavioral assessment using an assessment tool called DISC that I could see how I differed from other people.

The DISC behavior profile has been used by over 50 million people to help determine their behavioral tendencies, for example, making decisions: quickly from the gut versus deliberately after examining all possibilities. It categorizes people using four distinct behavioral styles and combinations of those four styles. The behaviors that are defined in this book as attributes to the HMHP are found in a combination of styles defined by the DISC assessment and my professional experience coaching managers to better understand them. Creative, visionary, focused, passionate, energetic, optimistic, risk taker, driver, influential, demanding, impatient, undetailed, direct, and charismatic are adjectives that describe them.

Because high-maintenance employees are so focused on goals and winning the race, they may believe that company rules don't apply to them. They only see what they think is important (sometimes less than a manager needs to make good decisions), they run around obstacles to get done faster, sometimes trampling over time-tested procedures, but they won't quit before the finish line—usually before the deadline and ahead of all others. Managers who are high-maintenance employees are visionary and love to generate new ideas and change how business gets done often without regard to the details for implementation and the subsequent consequences for those around them. They are all about business and getting the job done and less likely to be social with those who work for them. They tend to take on or initiate more projects, work longer hours, and get more done than other managers, and are often seen as pacesetters unconcerned about quality of life issues.

Properly managed high-maintenance employees excel; improperly managed they are often difficult, demanding, and disruptive in the workforce.

In the upcoming chapters you will learn how to:
- Recognize these next generation leaders.
- Foster their job satisfaction and performance.
- Hold them accountable for company directed results.

CHAPTER 1

Identifying and Appreciating High-Maintenance High Performers

*"Only positive consequences
encourage good future performance."*
—Ken Blanchard

Reading this chapter you will learn about:
- Characteristics of HMHPs
- The value of HMHPs in successful companies
- How learning about behavioral attributes can help HMHPs be more productive and easier to manage

Joe has been the senior vice president of a successful manufacturing company for many years. He is a brilliant man. Many call him a visionary. He has the ideas his company needs to propel it through tight competitive maneuvers or economic downturns. When a situation calls for action, Joe gives his staff outstanding solutions to implement. They say, "We've got to do this, because that's how he says it needs to be done."

On the surface this appears to be a winning combination: brilliant leadership and followers accomplishing brilliant results.

The undercurrent in this environment, however, is divisive. Joe doesn't know it, but his people perceive him as arrogant, demanding, and egotistical. His staff members do not see him as approachable, nor do they feel he is open to ideas that differ from his own.

Joe, on the other hand, hasn't developed meaningful relationships with his people and can't make the connections to get the feedback he needs from them. He doesn't even know they aren't being open and honest with him.

These characteristics and the reaction of Joe's staff are not unusual. In fact, they are typical of some of the most successful managers in some of the most successful companies.

Even though Joe has brilliant ideas, his leadership style is not effective. His style results in a high turnover rate for his team, which is costing his company a fortune.

Clearly, Joe is having trouble communicating with his staff. He is not good at relating to people. He isn't empowering his managers and other staff to be innovative. Although he has the right ideas to help lead the company to great heights, his leadership is compromised. His inability to develop meaningful relationships with his staff and receive feedback results in divisions within his team. Implementing solutions, no matter how brilliant, without a circular information flow also opens his company to the possibility of unanticipated, maybe even disastrous results. When things fail in that way, a typical response is, "Well, that's what you told me to do."

Characteristics of the High-Maintenance Employee

We often label people who operate like Joe as high performers. Because they are so results driven, they often complete significantly more work than their counterparts. In this book, I go one step further; I call them high-maintenance employees. By high maintenance, I mean they take more effort to manage and there is a greater risk that they will fail—in a big way. They are not interested in the details, yet they demand that things get done exactly their way.

Have you ever dealt with someone so caught up in his own ideas that he couldn't see any other way of doing something? After trying to reason with him, you probably felt as though this individual had sucked the life right out of you.

As you will see, the more misunderstood and mismanaged these high-maintenance employees are, the more difficult they are to manage and the more disruptive they are to an organization's overall effectiveness.

High-maintenance employees are goal focused. Some of the adjectives that describe them include: visionary, charismatic, focused on task, direct, and driving. On the downside, HMHPs also can be confrontational, demanding, impatient, and blunt. They may lack empathy and are not detail-oriented.

Despite their charisma, they are not people-oriented. Because they tend to become department or division leaders, presidents, or CEOs, their lack of attention to social interaction often becomes an obstacle as they usually need to work through others in order to get results.

Because they are results–driven, high-maintenance employees are demanding. A sure sign that you are dealing with HMHPs is the way in which they make demands on themselves and others. Here are some comments that typify how high-maintenance employees talk:

- "I don't care how you do it; I just want it done; I want it done now."
- "Can't you make an exception for me?"
- "Let's try this new idea that I have..."
- "Get out of my way so I can get it done."
- "No excuses."
- "I needed that yesterday."
- "Don't do tomorrow what you can do today."
- "What do you mean, no?"

A common misperception about high-maintenance employees is that they require a great deal of direction. High-maintenance employees need only enough direction to be sure they know what result is required in a given situation. As visionaries and big-picture thinkers, they need only enough direction to allow them to fly. Even when you give them direction, they need to perceive they still have the freedom to soar on their own.

On the other hand, they need to be trained to behave like a hawk. They must know to come back to earth after soaring to the great heights where they develop their visionary ideas and solutions. Once back, they will drive those ideas to the finish line, not just to finish the project successfully, but also because they want to get to the next big project, where they can let their intellectual prowess take flight again.

One reason people perceive high-maintenance employees as impossible to manage is their tendency to get bored easily. To manage high-maintenance employees effectively, you need to make sure they know that when they finish one project, another challenge lies ahead. Many high-maintenance employees thrive in entrepreneurial companies because of the sense of independence, freedom, and new challenges this type of environment usually embodies.

That doesn't mean that high-maintenance employees don't value working under good leadership or being a leader. Typically, however, being the leader is not a motivator for them. Often the motivation comes from their drive to succeed, the motivation to achieve self-actualization and, conversely, their fear of failing.

They have little tolerance for people who move slower than they do or who don't quickly get to the bottom line in conversation. That's why they are more successful working in an environment that allows them independence and room for innovation, with little need for rules and procedures that slow them down.

In working for others, they need to feel as though they are operating a business within a business. The more responsible they feel for the success and failure of their business within a business, the more likely they are to take complete ownership. Once they are committed, they take what they do very seriously.

High-maintenance employees will tend to operate according to their own standards and what they think is the "right" way to do things. They are visionary and when they decide they want to do something they will drive to achieve the results. Expect them to return another day when they hear no for an answer. They will attempt to side step the rules in an effort to achieve.

Why Companies Need HMHPs

At a leadership conference I attended in New York City, a number of high-profile chief executives talked about how they operate in the CEO role as well as their views on the attributes that are important for leaders to have. I was impressed by how often their descriptions and characterizations were closely aligned with those of high-maintenance employees. They provided valuable insight into how important these individuals can be for companies as well as some of the pitfalls they encounter if they aren't aware of their weaknesses and how to compensate for them.

For example, Rudy Giuliani, mayor of New York City during the 9/11 attack, said that as a leader he tends to make decisions quickly. Consequently, he learned to slow down and be more contemplative. He did this by surrounding himself with process-oriented people who tended to make decisions based on a lot of data or by looking from many angles at the consequences of decisions.

Jack Welch, former CEO of General Electric, talked about the importance for leaders to surround themselves with people who can give "direct appraisals." HMHPs are noted for being direct, and they need people around them who can be equally direct in their feedback.

Companies with high-maintenance employees like Joe, who I described at the start of this chapter, are more likely to respond quickly to changing environments. With high-maintenance employees, a company can drive to results more quickly: create, build, ship products, and close business.

High-maintenance employees tend not to give up before reaching their goal. Individuals who are the slower, steady type of performer or those who analyze each situation in detail are more likely to give up. The words "can't do" are not part of the high-maintenance employees vocabulary. If they believe in a goal, they will be relentless in coming up with a way, and often a better way, to achieve it. High-maintenance employees will achieve their goals, often before they are expected to achieve them. Creating an environment that encourages the strengths of high-maintenance employees is like striking gold.

High-maintenance employees are the change agents. They are those that will lead you or your team to make innovative changes in the organization. They are the creative problem solvers always looking for ways to make things better. They will forge ahead implementing and executing new ideas and new ways of thinking.

Smart companies are always looking at ways to improve how their people get work done, cultivating their next leaders, and looking for visionaries who can produce results. Thus, smart companies should always look for high-maintenance employees.

How Examining Behaviors Improves Teamwork

Now that you know about some of the benefits of high-maintenance employees, how do you get them to interact as a part of your team? Understanding the way HMHPs operate can help make them more productive. The following story is a great example. One of my clients had a number of HMHPs on his sales teams. Tim is vice president of one of the largest manufacturing companies on the East Coast. He called me and said, "Kathi, help! I am having problems managing my teams. My sales staff is arrogant, demanding, and egotistical. They are driving me crazy." Tim felt frustrated and irritated because he just wasn't getting the results he needed from his top performers. He felt like a failure... not a manager.

After several hours of discussion, I suggested we work on three main areas: communicating, motivating, and developing top performers. We interviewed his sales staff and had all team members complete a behavioral profile, called DISC, to identify their natural behavioral tendencies. A behavioral profile helps to identify the differences in how people like to operate, their natural tendencies for communicating and executing projects, and other characteristics.

During this process of assessing the behavioral characteristics for each individual, we found that the team members Tim was most concerned about were HMHPs. They were very intense and extremely task focused. They operated independently of the team. If Tim offered information that had no direct impact on them—including meetings, associated projects, or any team-oriented action items—they didn't want to get involved. This resulted in a lack of communication within their teams.

Through executive coaching, we worked with Tim on how to take a very logical, unemotional approach to handling his team members, especially the HMHPs who were causing him the most grief. One of the things he did was to put the HMHPs in charge of a team. Being in charge of a team meant driving the team goals and being placed in a situation where they could lead and have some control over achieving the results.

Tim also created some simple processes and structures to give the teams the support they needed from other departments. For example, before creating the new structure, it was impossible to get results accomplished through the other departments. Tim worked with the other department heads, who in turn assigned point people to communicate with Tim's team.

So what happened? What Tim had called teams really turned into teams. They worked cohesively, they were not divided, and they all had the same goals. According to Tim, once he discovered what his HMHPs really needed and gave it to them, "the results were phenomenal."

By understanding what they needed, Tim created an environment for the HMHPs where they could realize their goals and operate efficiently. As their boss, he ran interference and removed roadblocks to their success.

Once you take the time to understand how your HMHPs behave and make a few minor adjustments to allow them to operate in an environment that supports their best work, you'll find that your top performers can also be easy to work with. They will be able to accomplish more, and you'll reap greater, long-lasting rewards.

Understanding Joe's Challenge

Joe knew he had to take action but he wasn't sure what to do. Fortunately, Joe's manager also contracted to provide him with executive coaching as part of a company leadership development program. With his coaching, Joe received feedback that he wasn't connecting with his staff. He learned that his staff felt he was unapproachable and that they feared that if they came to Joe with a problem, he might talk down to them.

Joe's manager knew he needed to reverse the negative opinions that Joe's employees had formed about him by helping Joe understand that others do not communicate or respond to communication the same way he does. For his part, Joe was hopeful that someone outside his organization could offer a fresh perspective.

How focusing on behavioral characteristics helped

In addition to coaching, Joe took the DISC behavioral assessment to help him profile his behavioral tendencies as well as another profile that included his values. The findings suggested that Joe is very task focused, likes challenges, and strives for success in everything he does...all admirable traits for a leader in a company in a highly competitive environment.

Joe, however, would often provide a solution rather than empower others to come up with one on their own. He rarely involved his team in the future planning of the division. The division often failed to complete what he started because Joe added more and more new projects without establishing any priority for delivering results.

Based on the analysis, Joe's action plan identified three main factors to work on. These were communicating (listening), motivating others, and developing people. These areas, again, are common challenges for HMHPs.

The implementation

What Joe discovered from the behavioral profiles made him realize how those who did not know him well could perceive him as distant and unapproachable. It became clearer why he felt so distant from his staff, and he could see the possible pitfalls of not having the information he needed to make the right decisions.

To make progress with his employees, Joe chose to focus on building relationships with them and on being more open-minded about how he handled his responsibilities.

With coaching, Joe developed a plan that included working with each person on his team. He began to recognize how others processed information, how he sometimes was an ineffective communicator, and ways he could communicate better with his direct staff and the managers who reported to him as well. Instead of saying, "Here's how you need to do it..." he asks, "What else can you do to rise above the circumstances and achieve the results you want?"

The results of behavioral profiling

After six months of coaching and follow-through on his plan, Joe said, "I wasn't sure what to expect. I was surprised to learn that by changing the way I approached the problem, I was able to get things done in a manner I would not have ordinarily tried. The training really helped me to approach some work relationships in new ways. I'm more effective at gaining cooperation from coworkers and I am able to do a better job of getting results by changing my approach."

This has been a quick look at the behaviors of the HMHP and at how adapting natural behavioral tendencies can transform relationships, and, more importantly, group and individual performance.

Moving Forward

In the coming chapters you will learn how to hire high-maintenance employees to enrich your employee mix, integrate them into teams, give them the freedom they need to perform, and train them to give you the accountability you need.

In this book, we will cover many aspects of managing HMHPs and their behaviors, as well as how to adapt other behavioral styles to communicate, motivate, and manage high-maintenance employees more effectively. I'll even cover what high-maintenance employees need to know about themselves and tips on working more effectively with a high-maintenance boss.

Behavioral profiles are an innovative way to discover individual and team strengths and weaknesses. They are powerful tools for analyzing why people behave, interact, and communicate the way they do. We will discuss behavioral profiling in the next chapter.

CHAPTER 2

Knowing Yourself and Those You Work With

"He who knows others is learned,
he who knows himself is wise."

—Lao Tse

In this chapter, you will learn:
- Why behavioral profiling is a key tool that can help you work effectively with HMHPs and others
- How to determine your own behavioral style
- The four primary behavioral styles

Good communication has long been a cornerstone of a successful business. Simply stated, it can make or break your organization. However, with the diverse array of communication styles, most businesses find it difficult to ascertain and implement strategically effective customer and employee communication systems.

Each person has a preferred style of giving and receiving information. The lack of understanding of these styles often causes delays, misconceptions, and even conflict. Discovering the differences and working with each individual's boundaries greatly helps smooth the flow of communication.

A major tool for learning about the differences in communication styles is behavioral profiling. Through behavioral profiling, you can learn the communication dos and don'ts for working effectively with anyone, including staff members, peers, and bosses. You can learn the best way to motivate and coach each person on your staff. In the recruiting process, behavior profiling can be used to determine which job candidates are most likely to fit in well with your company's culture and with your team. Finally, by learning more about your own behavior style, you can identify tendencies that may be holding you back or strengths that you can build on to push toward success.

Behavioral Profiling in Action

People tend to hire people for technical skills (because they can actually do the job), but fire them for lack of soft skills (in other words, their attitudes stink). What behavioral profiling helps identify are the soft skills: the behaviors, attitudes, and values that influence how a person acts in the job.

After using a behavioral assessment tool for a year, a VP and sales manager told me why she thought the tool is valuable: "It is valuable first as a hiring tool, because it provides me with the information on the skills and traits that an individual has and their strengths and weaknesses. After an individual is hired, it also assists me in determining the best ways in which to communicate with that individual—what not to say, what to say, and how to say it."

One of her top sellers, a HMHP, took the behavioral profile for a test drive before the VP and I started working together. After we reviewed the results, the VP told me, "Kathi, it matches her style perfectly."

At the time, this seller had been on the VP's staff for two years, so the VP had had a lot of time to observe her behavior. The behavioral profile gave her manager subtle tips as to how to communicate with her more effectively.

With the information learned from the behavioral profile, the VP was able to take a great and growing seller and turn her, within a year, into one of the top sellers in the entire company. The seller has now, two years later, done more new business than any other sales person in the region.

It is important to understand the behaviors of those you manage, especially HMHPs, because they tend to be the most difficult employees to manage. Knowing the behavioral tendencies of a person can help you coach them to reach the next level in performance. While this book is about HMHPs, it is also valuable to have an overview of other behavioral types and how they interact with HMHPs.

One of the most widely used behavioral profiling tools, and one that I frequently use with clients, is the DISC profile. It is based on William Moulton Marston's Emotions of Normal People, which he wrote in 1928. More recently, other theorists have also described predominant behavioral tendencies in four categories. Carl Jung, for example, used sensing, intuitive, feeling, and thinking. Marston, however, may have been the first to use the four-category model to describe behaviors of normal people. At first, his DISC assessment was mostly used by the U.S. Army for recruiting but is now used extensively by the general population.

Several versions of the DISC profile are available on the market today, including online versions that are quick and easy to use.

The DISC language is based on observable behavior. The DISC model analyzes behavioral style; that is, a person's manner of doing things. It provides a way for you to assess the various ways people behave under certain circumstances, their motivators, their most natural attributes, their behavior in the work environment, and their preferred communication styles.

The DISC model is a development tool as well; it helps people learn how to communicate, interact, and manage their communications. While individuals cannot change their personalities, they can learn to change the way they behave to improve their communication and relationships with others, especially with those who have different behavioral styles.

DISC is also used as a team building tool. It helps individuals understand the strengths that they bring to their team individually and collectively. It can be used as a work flow design and implementation tool to help organizations capitalize on the collective strengths of their teams.

This has been a very quick review of the different behavioral styles. To obtain a much more detailed analysis of your own behavioral style, visit www.xbcoaching.com. The twenty-three-page report that results from taking the survey will give you a detailed analysis of your behavioral tendencies.

Determine Your Behavioral Style

To give you a better understanding of how behavioral profiling works, here is a short survey to help you identify some of the behavioral tendencies you may exhibit. Each of the four boxes below contains twenty adjectives. Think how each of the adjectives describes you. Check all that apply to you in each section. Then count the checks in each box. The highest total is usually the one that best describes you. Although your scores may be close in more than one part, most people have personal styles that match just one (or two, but rarely all four). The behavioral styles, as defined by the DISC model, are described in the section following the survey.

The DISC behavioral styles

DISC is an acronym for Dominance, Influence, Steadiness, and Compliance (or Conscience, in some versions of DISC that are on the market today). These are the four core behaviors that all people can be categorized by. There are, by all means, many combinations of the four styles, and that is what makes us all unique. Match the box you and your employee scored highest on in the survey with the descriptions below.

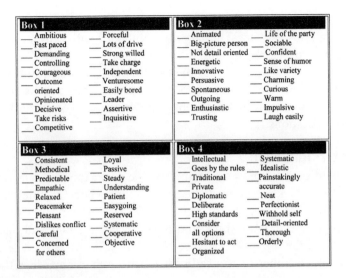

Box 1	
___ Ambitious	___ Forceful
___ Fast paced	___ Lots of drive
___ Demanding	___ Strong willed
___ Controlling	___ Take charge
___ Courageous	___ Independent
___ Outcome	___ Venturesome
oriented	___ Easily bored
___ Opinionated	___ Leader
___ Decisive	___ Assertive
___ Take risks	___ Inquisitive
___ Competitive	

Box 2	
___ Animated	___ Life of the party
___ Big-picture person	___ Sociable
___ Not detail oriented	___ Confident
___ Energetic	___ Sense of humor
___ Innovative	___ Like variety
___ Persuasive	___ Charming
___ Spontaneous	___ Curious
___ Outgoing	___ Warm
___ Enthusiastic	___ Impulsive
___ Trusting	___ Laugh easily

Box 3	
___ Consistent	___ Loyal
___ Methodical	___ Passive
___ Predictable	___ Steady
___ Empathic	___ Understanding
___ Relaxed	___ Patient
___ Peacemaker	___ Easygoing
___ Pleasant	___ Reserved
___ Dislikes conflict	___ Systematic
___ Careful	___ Cooperative
___ Concerned	___ Objective
for others	

Box 4	
___ Intellectual	___ Systematic
___ Goes by the rules	___ Idealistic
___ Traditional	___ Painstakingly
___ Private	accurate
___ Diplomatic	___ Neat
___ Deliberate	___ Perfectionist
___ High standards	___ Withhold self
___ Consider	___ Detail-oriented
all options	___ Thorough
___ Hesitant to act	___ Orderly
___ Organized	

Box 1: Dominance

Individuals who show a high Dominance style are those who tend to process quickly and are focused on tasks. These individuals tend to be results-oriented, focused on challenge and power, and like to make decisions quickly with confidence. They are the team members who you know will get the job done.

Some descriptors of this style include: driving, demanding, aggressive, pioneering, and competitive. They prefer to be evaluated on the results and not the process. They are goal driven and enjoy a personal challenge.

When you receive communication from someone who is high in Dominance, it could appear short, undetailed, overpowering, intimidating, insensitive to feelings, or exhibit a lack of patience. You may need to ask for additional information, as Dominance types often communicate in short bursts.

Team members who are Dominance-oriented will be at their best when solving problems and driving for results. They are positive, powerful, and authoritative. Dominance-oriented team members, however, will not be shy to overstep boundaries and use fear as a motivator. Further, they are known for their lack of listening skills and tact. They are often unhappy with routine work; they also over-delegate, and under-instruct.

If you think you fall into the Dominance category, you would help the communications process by improving your listening skills, being more patient, toning down directness, and asking more questions.

Box 2: Influence

Individuals who show a high Influence style are those who tend to process quickly and are focused on people. They are the team members who keep things exciting and keep everyone motivated. Recognition, relationships, and freedom from details will likely motivate them.

Team members who use Influence more than any other trait will need to be given time to socialize and lighten up. Not afraid to have fun, they ask for feelings and opinions, and they often show their best work during brainstorming sessions.

Influencers have a need to verbalize. They also lack attention to detail, appear superficial, have poor follow-through, and can appear manipulative. Influencers most likely will talk around a subject until they are able to make their point. You may find yourself exercising a lot of patience with Influencers.

Influencers are socially and verbally aggressive; they bring optimism, and have good persuasion skills and a vision of the big picture. They are people-oriented and team-oriented. Individuals who exhibit Influence are impulsive and unrealistic in appraising people, and they often cannot pay attention to detail, and are frequently disorganized.

If you are an Influencer, you can improve your communication with others by listening to the real needs of the person with whom you are speaking, being more organized, and being specific in direction and praise.

Box 3: Steadiness

Individuals who show a high Steadiness style tend to process more methodically and are focused on people. These individuals tend to be loyal, cooperative, calm, and methodical in how they deal with life. They are the team members who make sure that everyone on the team is doing okay. Security, stability, and sincere appreciation will likely motivate them.

Those whose core communication style is Steadiness are often described as: adaptable, systematic, unhurried, predictable, and consistent.

Their needs-driven behavior is accommodation, and they also possess a need to be of help to others. When you communicate with someone who exhibits high Steadiness, you will want to be patient, draw out their opinion, provide a logical approach to the facts, relax, and allow time for discussion, show how a solution would benefit them, clearly define all areas and involve them in the planning stage.

When you receive communication from someone with a core Steadiness style, it may appear non-emotional, indecisive, too indirect, and lacking in assertiveness. It may also seem as though they are providing an enormous amount of detail.

Steady team members are loyal to those they identify with; they are good listeners, they are patient and empathetic. High-Steadiness individuals are limited in that they tend to get in a rut, they resist change, and they hold grudges. They don't project a sense of urgency and are low-risk takers.

If you are a Steadiness type, to communicate more effectively you could improve your assertiveness skills, stop taking on the problems of others, and embrace change to help with communication.

Box 4: Compliance

Individuals who show a high Compliance style tend to process more methodically and are focused on tasks. These individuals tend to be analytical and precise. They value quality and accuracy on a project. They are the team members who keep standards high and pay attention to details. Professional standards, defined expectations, and a quality focus will likely motivate them.

These are the rule followers. Individuals high in Compliance are painstaking, wary, meticulous, quality-conscious, and perfectionistic. Their two primary driving forces are following the rules and complying with their own high standards.

To successfully communicate with high-Compliance types, use data and facts, and examine the argument from all sides. Keep on the task—don't socialize. If your opinion differs from that of a high-Compliance individual, disagree with the facts, not the person. These individuals will be best satisfied if you focus on quality by avoiding new solutions and sticking with proven ideas.

When receiving information from someone high in Compliance, it could seem excessive. They tend to appear as perfectionists, coming across as aloof, too rule-focused, critical, and slow to proceed; bear with them. They must process the information before being able to communicate their ideas. High-Compliance individuals give their best to the team in the areas of critical thinking. However, they hesitate to act without precedent and are bound by procedures. Typically, they do not take risks or verbalize feelings, and they avoid controversy.

If you feel you fall into the Compliance style, consider improving your patience, building more rapport, allowing more gray area, and being more accepting of differences.

The Behavioral Style of HMHPs

The DISC analysis has so many possible combinations that it is impossible to predict exactly what each person's behavioral style is. It is only possible to talk about tendencies and preferences. But it is truly remarkable how much can be predicted from the assessment when it comes to HMHPs.

Most HMHPs will tend to have a primary Dominance behavioral style. Not all people high on the Dominance scale are

HMHPs. Those with the high Dominance characteristics who are HMHPs may also be high or low in Influence, but typically are low in Steadiness and Compliance. Research conducted by Target Training International via a random sample approximately every three years has found that about 18 percent of the U.S. population has a primary Dominance style. Keep in mind that this percentage varies from industry to industry and within various professions.

All people are not the same. A strategy that is very effective with one person can be disastrous with another. Learning by trial and error about which strategies are most effective with which people can be very costly in time, money, and emotional energy. By using the DISC system or another behavioral profiling tool for managing others, you can use less of all three valuable resources.

Understanding Behavioral Styles Achieves Better Results

Here is an example of how one manager worked with an individual on her team who has a Steadiness and Compliance behavioral style. Knowing about the different behavioral styles helped her to use a behavioral style that best suited each person for achieving the end results.

When asked to plan the training that was needed for her team, Mary, who was a high-maintenance employee, responded by creating the objectives for her team for the entire year and a description of how each new training topic would build on the previous topic. In addition, she created what outcomes should be achieved for each individual session. Mary's strength is creating the results. She can take a problem and create a strategy that will get her the outcome she desires.

After she completed the objectives, she gave them to George, one of the managers who reported to her.

George is detailed and methodical in his approach to dealing with problems. George, with a Steadiness style, created the process for each objective/training session and how it would be delivered to the team. He created specific steps to accomplish the objectives that Mary outlined. He chose the individuals who would deliver the training and the dates for each session. George also created a plan to follow up on a regular basis on how the team was using the new behaviors and information they learned.

In this case, Mary created the objectives that would get to the results, using her strengths, and George created the step-by-step plan using his strengths.

Moving Forward

You can become more effective in working with others by using a behavioral style that is based on recognizing and respecting individual differences with regard to communication and other key behaviors. The first step in knowing what works best with different individuals is to obtain behavioral profiles using one of the many profiling tools available, including the popular DISC model.

Behavior profiles can help you bring the right people into your organization and develop them so that they achieve their full potential and drive your business forward. Knowledge of behavioral styles and preferences is essential to team building since individuals who truly understand each other can work more cohesively and with less friction than those who aren't aware of individual differences in communication preferences and other behaviors.

Finally, by learning more about your own behavioral style, you can become a more effective leader, manager, and team member.

CHAPTER 3

Understanding the High-Maintenance, High Performer Communication Style

"Eloquence is the power to translate a truth into language perfectly intelligible to the person to whom you speak."

—Ralph Waldo Emerson

In this chapter, you will learn:
- Strategies for effective communication with HMHPs
- The importance of directness when communicating with HMHPs
- The differences in written communication intended for HMHPs and their non–HMHP counterparts

People are who they are due to a complex mixture of experience, heredity, and self-discovery. These elements (and more) combine to create a person's communication style, attitudes, interests, behavioral style, and values. To understand your HMHPs, you must first understand their makeup.

As you have learned in Chapter 2, "Identifying and Appreciating High-maintenance High Performers," understanding the behavior of these hard-driving individuals is a powerful tool in managing them. Exactly how do you use the DISC or any behavioral tool to understand the communication style of your HMHPs? First, let's look at what the DISC behavioral tool measures.

As described in Chapter 3, the DISC behavioral model helps to define observed behavior. It provides a way for you to assess the various ways people behave under certain circumstances: their motivators, their most natural attributes, their behavior in the work environment, and their preferred communication styles.

Each person has a preferred style of giving and receiving information. The lack of understanding of these styles often causes delays, misconceptions, and even conflict. Discovering the differences and working with their boundaries greatly helps in smoothing the flow of communication. Since HMHPs have the potential to be the strongest contributors to your organization's success, it is particularly important to understand their communication preferences.

One of the defining characteristics of HMHPs is that they want to do things their way. This trait shows through in their communication style. A good example of the HMHP communication style was exhibited in the movie *When Harry Met Sally*. Remember the restaurant scene when Sally was ordering? She'd say things like, "I'll have the chicken Caesar salad with the chicken well-done, the croutons on the side, no tomatoes, extra cheese, and instead of Caesar dressing I'll have ranch...on the side." She had her own ideas. She knew precisely what she wanted, and she asked for it. Sally was definitely high maintenance.

Communicating Information to the Different Styles

In the same way you decide what vehicle to use for delivering information, whether by telephone, email, proposal, report, or oral presentation, understanding how to communicate so the various behavioral styles are more receptive to it will also improve communication. So it's important to understand the best way to deliver information for the different styles, both high-maintenance and non-HMHPs. Here are ways to improve communication with the various behavioral styles.

When using email with a HMHP, use bulleted points, be brief, and focus on results and benefits, then summarize the bottom line results. Use a positive introduction. You want to highlight the benefits and generate excitement. Similar strategies can be used for reporting or delivering an oral presentation to the HMHP. When making a presentation, you want to be fast and focus on the business results. Use colorful visuals and bring a sample if it's appropriate.

In contrast, with individuals who exhibit the non-HMHP attributes, when you email, use a friendly introduction and outline the service or product in a step-by-step process. Use a formal approach. Attach any details. When you write a proposal to someone with this style, you want to outline the products and services in detail and attach supporting materials if possible, including references. Be accurate and detailed and provide research or statistics about the products and services. In a live presentation, you want to be friendly and sincere, use team language, and leave time for review. Be formal and courteous and be accurate. Use graphs and charts where appropriate.

The following chart shows in more detail how the key behavioral styles prefer to receive communication.

	Email	Proposal	Presentation
Dominance	• Use bullets • Be brief • Focus on results and benefits	• Use bullets • Highlight benefits • Summarize bottom-line results	• Be fast • Focus on business results
Influence	• Use positive introduction • Highlight benefits and generate excitement	• Use colorful visuals • Bring sample if appropriate • Summarize benefits to people	• Be friendly and positive • Break the ice • Be brief and fast
Steadiness	• Use friendly introduction • Outline service or product in a step-by-step process	• Outline products and services in detail • Attach supporting materials if possible • Include references	• Be friendly and sincere • Leave time for review • Use team language
Compliance	• Use formal approach • Get right to the point • Attach details	• Be accurate and detailed • Provide statistics or research about products/services	• Be formal and courteous • Be accurate • Use graphs and charts

Sample Email
to High-Maintenance Employees

Using the guidelines given in this chapter for communicating with HMHPs, here is an example of how to write an effective email message.

```
Hi everyone,
Attached are the updates and changes to the manual. We
want to get this out to the team as quickly as possible so
we can clear up any challenges the team has been having.
Please forward any changes or additions to me by tomorrow
afternoon.
Look at any areas that are blank and provide your
feedback.
I will make the corrections and send them back to you.

Thanks for all your hard work and dedication to this
project.
Mary
```

Sample Email
for Non-High-Maintenance Employees

In contrast, here is how the Steadiness style would prefer to receive information.

```
Hi everyone,
Here are the updates and changes to the manual. Chris,
thank you for forwarding the job descriptions for all the
positions. As I was reviewing them, I realized that in
adding all that info it would cause us to have to go
back and re-do the "time required" information in a very
in-depth way. We have defined these specific tasks in
much broader categories and it seems to me that most of
the specific tasks are included in the broader cate-
gories. Please review the training needs that we defined
yesterday. Feel free to add what you feel is important
from the job descriptions that is not already included in
```

the categories we listed. I will then add those missing
pieces to the training need lists. I think this will be
the best way to handle this.

There are a few blank areas under the "time required to
learn" that we didn't define yesterday. Some areas will
be blank if they already have experience and don't need
training. Any feedback that you have here would be
appreciated.

There are a few other areas we will need to clarify on
page 22 dealing with Performance Issues and
Gossip/Negative Talk that Chris brought forward. We will
be sure to define those with you more clearly before we
finalize the manual. I just wanted Chris to know we
haven't forgotten them!
Thanks for all your hard work and dedication to this
project.
Mary

The differences in these two communication approaches are
easy to see. Both communication styles are effective when used
with the matching personality type. But using the wrong style
with HMHPs can be disastrous. Succinct communication with
value, especially if it is tied to the bottom line or their success, is
extremely important for your HMHPs

Winning Strategies for Communicating with HMHPs

Here are three key strategies you can use in understanding the
high performer communication style.

Coach or guide, don't tell.

Many managers of high-maintenance employees make the mistake of telling rather than guiding. Often it is simply a matter of
how a request is phrased. Having been a HMHP all of my life, I
had many experiences with managers who would lead by telling. I

had an experience with one manager who would continually ask me to take his step-by-step approach. But I often thought of several other ways that projects and people should be dealt with. We would get into disagreements on a regular basis about doing things "his way." High-maintenance employees really dislike being told what to do.

We both would have had a lot more peace if he could have given me a little freedom—perhaps by allowing me to accomplish tasks in one of several different ways. When you communicate with your HMHPs, don't prescribe to them. Give them options. Remember, they like the freedom to operate in their own way.

Chapter 8 provides detailed strategies for specific management skills and coaching techniques.

Be direct, specific, brief, and to the point.

High-maintenance employees are probably the most impatient people you will ever meet. They exhibit their impatience in almost everything that they do. This is how most high-maintenance employees performers perceive the rest of the world. Anything other than the matter at hand is heard as "blah, blah, blah."

High-maintenance employees appreciate small talk. (Notice I said "appreciate" not "participate in freely.") And they chitchat from time to time. However, always in the back of their minds is the thought, "Let's get on with it!"

As results-oriented people, they are ready to see the bottom line. They want to go for the gold right now. Once they're done, then there will be time for small talk. Tell them what they need to know and turn them loose! If they believe in a goal, they will be relentless in coming up with a way to achieve it. High-maintenance employees will achieve, or exceed their goals, often before they are expected to achieve them.

Don't talk about rules and restrictions.

HMHPs don't like being told what they can't do. If you need to change the direction in which a HMHP is charging, then use coaching language to help them understand the consequences. Imposing rules will only challenge them to overcome the obstacles. They want the freedom to run their own projects and construct their own plan to get there. They don't like to be asked how they got to the end result, just whether or not they go there.

Difficult Management Communication Styles for HMHPs

Communicating with a high-maintenance employee requires a very different approach. By understanding the behavioral styles of others as well as your own, you can adapt the way in which you communicate with your high-maintenance employees to meet their needs and get the results you want. Here's how one manager was able to adapt to get results from his HMHPs. Based on the findings of a behavioral assessment profile, Bob discovered he was high in the Steadiness behavioral style, clearly a non-high-maintenance employee. As a leader, Bob likes to process information before he makes decisions. He takes a methodical approach when making decisions and does not make decisions based on emotions. He is most comfortable with others who do not operate emotionally and who consider the facts before taking action.

Most people on the sales staff, however, had high-maintenance tendencies, the opposite of his behavioral style.

To overcome the challenge of communication with his sales team, Bob first had to understand how and why both he and the salespeople communicated in the way they did. That knowledge would be the foundation for how Bob could adapt his style to the way his sales force receives information and uses the information to take action.

Instead of stating every step of his information-gathering process to a salesperson who is high maintenance, he relayed the information in such a way that the employee could see the end results. Instead of giving what the salesperson would perceive as endless or painful detail, he presented bullet points, something high-maintenance employees prefer.

In addition, Bob began to understand that some previous negative statements or behaviors from sales team members were not necessarily as bad as they appeared. For example, the sales team wanted answers right away. They became pushy or irritated if they had to wait to get answers or information. On the other hand, Bob was cautious in his approach. He wanted to make sure he had the correct information before he gave an answer.

Over time, Bob gained an entirely new understanding of others' behavioral styles and preferences in communication. He got back to the sales team members right away even if he didn't have the answer. He communicated on his progress or his thoughts on a regular basis and he always followed up in a timely manner. This in turn helped Bob become more effective and less stressed at the office.

As Bob and his team demonstrate, the most troubling communication styles for the HMHP are the core high Steadiness and the core high Compliance behavioral styles or a combination of these styles. Someone with a high Steadiness style tends to be well organized and puts structure to ideas. They are also consistent, industrious, serious, and methodical. They also like stability and want to be part of the team. They tend to be supportive, helpful, and dependable.

The reason non-high-maintenance employees behavioral styles tend to be more challenging for high-maintenance employees is in part due to how quickly high-maintenance employees prefer to make decisions. High-maintenance employees prefer a fast pace. They like to move quickly in most everything that they do. They tend to be extroverted, outgoing, and verbal. They are motivated by results, by creativity, and go by their gut and what feels right. They get very frustrated by obstacles that may prevent them from getting what they want. They have little concern about the process even if they are knowledgeable about what the process should be. They like the freedom to create new approaches.

Add this all together and you have an individual who has little patience for people who exhibit other behavioral styles. If the person in charge falls into the non-high-maintenance group, then this may be particularly frustrating for high-maintenance employees, who can view this individual as a major roadblock to their forward progress.

Non-high-maintenance managers tend to be very strategic by nature. They like the planning and they are good at it. They need to understand how all of the pieces in the process are going to be connected to the outcome. And our HMHPs are saying, "Don't worry about it; just let me go. I can get this done. I'm optimistic, I'm positive that I know this is the 'right' thing to do."

Whereas, the non-high-maintenance employee takes a much more methodical approach. These leaders want everything in order. They are extremely organized; they tend to be very detailed in their approach to decision making and planning. They tend to like things in writing. They like supporting data or supporting detail.

Communication Strategy Summary

In summary, here are important strategies you can use in communicating with HMHPs to reduce miscommunication and limit their frustration.

- Focus on the task and stick to business.
- Take a results-oriented, logical approach.
- Identify opportunities or challenges.
- Provide a win-win situation.
- Ask for their feelings and opinions.
- Involve them in brainstorming.

Moving Forward

By being aware of the huge contribution high-maintenance employees can make to your organization's success, you should be motivated to move beyond your comfort zone and develop ways of communicating with these individuals that help them get the great results they are capable of achieving.

How you communicate with high-maintenance employees can make a world of difference between whether they are successful and content in their positions or whether they feel constrained and frustrated. By speaking in a coaching style instead of an authoritarian style, by being direct and succinct and by imposing as few rules as possible, you'll inspire your high-maintenance employees to new heights.

At the same time, it's important to understand that your non-high-maintenance employees need more direction and detail and a friendlier approach that supports their need for a feeling of camaraderie.

In subsequent chapters, I'll talk about how the drive of these highly-motivated individuals can be harnessed to better facilitate their interactions with non-high-maintenance employees, how to integrate them as part of a team, and how to manage them.

CHAPTER 4

Creating the Right Environment for High-Maintenance Employees

"Nothing great was ever achieved without enthusiasm."

—Ralph Waldo Emerson

Read this chapter to learn about:
- The importance of environment for high-maintenance employees
- Creating an environment that fosters high performance
- Environments that motivate high-maintenance employees

Many leaders talk to me about how they are challenged in finding top performers. Because of the competitive nature of business today, it's also hard to keep them once you've found them. Most high-maintenance employees have many options in the business world that are being presented to them on a regular basis. They also like new experiences. So they tend to be open to new possibilities in the job market.

Environments That Take a Personal Interest

If you want to keep your high-maintenance employees challenged, it is critical to create an environment where they can thrive.

Here are some ideas on how to create this environment:

1. Teach your business to your high-maintenance employees.

As visionaries, high-maintenance employees do best and are most content when they understand how their own actions impact the overall success of the business. This principle takes your employees beyond just doing their jobs.

Constantly communicate your mission and vision and make sure your high-maintenance employees know where they fit into that mission and vision. Open your books and be willing to talk specifics about the direction your company is going. When they understand the big picture, high-maintenance employees will use their drive to help take your company where you want to go.

2. Practice the platinum rule.

Go beyond the Golden Rule. Don't treat people the way you want to be treated; treat them the way they want to be treated.

Every person you employ is different. Don't force them to fit a mold. Don't make assumptions. Take time to ask your high-maintenance employees what they want, how they prefer to communicate, which rewards mean the most to them, and what their aspirations are. Recognize their accomplishments and contributions. High-maintenance performers enjoy being told that they have done exceptional work. They like to feel as though they are leading the pack through their own accomplishments. This is in part due to their ego drive and in part because of their competitive nature. Make employee recognition a strong part of your company culture. Make sure your high-maintenance performers know where they are making a difference and that you're paying attention to them. They like attention. They like to know that they are important and that their contributions do matter, probably more so than your non-high-maintenance employees. High-maintenance employees like recognition and they like it publicly. Make sure you acknowledge innovative things that they do that make a difference. Run the acknowledgement up the chain of command so those individuals who are important to the organization see the acknowledgment and contributions. Send your high-maintenance employees notes thanking them for their contributions. Acknowledging how they are contributing is a way of keeping them engaged and contributing.

3. Get to know your high-maintenance employees as more than employees.

There should never be an instance where you approach one of your high-maintenance employees in the hallway and think "Oh... what is her name again?" High-maintenance employees want to know that they are making a difference. They want others in the organization to know who they are and the contributions they make.

Not only do you want to make sure you know every one of your high-maintenance employees by name and recognize their contributions publicly, it also pays to get to know them outside the office. You'd be amazed at what insights their "alter egos" can provide you with. By taking time to establish relationships with them that go deeper than just manager/employee, you can learn what makes them tick and pick up information that will help you create the work atmosphere that fits them best.

4. Leverage the power of a buddy system, especially for new hires.

Use only high-maintenance employees who already work for you to mentor your new high-maintenance employees. Such a mentoring program is a great way to introduce people to your organization and this style of learning—which focuses on showing instead of telling—particularly fits with the HMHP personality. Having mentors gives your new high-maintenance employees a safe way to ask confidential questions, look beyond written policy and procedure manuals, and find their place within your organization much more quickly than if left to fly solo.

5. Have fun at work!

When you incorporate fun and creativity in the workplace, you build an atmosphere in which innovation flows freely. Since this is exactly what high-maintenance employees excel at, they love such environments.

Take field trips. Create a room filled with toys that employees can play with (video games are usually a big hit). After all, have you ever heard of an employee leaving a job that was fun and paid well? Make sure these activities are directly tied to the results your high-maintenance employees are trying to achieve.

6. Communicate clearly at all times.

Don't assume your high-maintenance employees know what is expected of them. Use the tools described in Chapter 7 on hiring to clearly outline job responsibilities, the measurements used for performance reviews, and give them the chain of command, among other things. High-maintenance employees will take initiative if not told what is expected of them. Defining this up front will reduce frustration for both you and your high-maintenance employees. Your high-maintenance employees will feel valued if you make sure they have exciting work to do. They want to feel a sense of accomplishment—a sense that they are really contributing. Set growth plans for your high-maintenance employees that provide them with new challenges, chances to learn new skills, and opportunities to lead. This is a sure-fire way to make sure your high-maintenance performers feel they are challenged and valued members of your organization.

7. Conduct exit interviews.

If you do lose a high-maintenance employee, you definitely want to know why. Conducting an exit interview will provide you with valuable information that may help you overcome problems that high-maintenance employees are encountering in your organization. Be prepared for the usual directness that high-maintenance employees are known for when you conduct this discussion. Do not be defensive about the information you hear. Instead, focus on what you can learn that will help in the future.

Creating a Motivating Work Environment

Here are characteristics of an environment that will improve job satisfaction for your high-maintenance employees:

1. Freedom to operate

Because the HMHP is goal-driven, achievement is a motivating factor. High-maintenance employees will thrive in an environment where they have freedom to operate. They will thrive because there is little structure around how something needs to get accomplished. In the case where you require some structure, give your high-maintenance employees options as to how they can achieve a goal.

They are motivated be developing the big picture idea. They tend to think in broader views and will serve you and your organization best if they are driving and executing their plan. Don't restrict them. Give them the flexibility and freedom to innovate. As their manager, you must be ready to run interference for them.

Given the freedom to choose how they accomplish their goals will often result in new ways—faster, more efficient, higher quality—of getting things done.

2. Freedom to lead

High-maintenance employees like to have control. They like to lead and direct. When involved in a project with a team, they will be inspired by taking on leadership roles. Give your high-maintenance employees the freedom to run their own projects. Allow them to execute on their own ideas for moving projects forward. These people are your drivers. Let them drive and you will see the results.

I was working for one of the major-market broadcast companies. I'd been working on my first project assignment for about three months when my boss asked to meet me for breakfast.

So I'm prepared. I've updated all of my projections, I have my plan. I know what to wear, what I'm going to order...

I'm thinking this is great. I have the plan. I'm ready—not just ready, I'm prepared—to meet with my boss. I can't wait to talk about my plan, my strategy.

The day comes; I'm dressed for business...I arrive...we meet...we sit down.

My boss speaks very slowly, not like he has trouble getting started in the morning, more as though he thinks about everything he says before he says it. He is very deliberate in everything he says, even the chitchat...he starts with some getting to know you better chitchat, you know how that goes...and more chitchat—but meanwhile I'm thinking to myself, get on with it...

He finishes the chitchat and the meeting starts. He starts telling me about a project I'm working on...I'm working on, not him... He asks me how I think it's going and I say great. I'm very excited about the challenge and the responsibility. And that's true. I'm feeling very optimistic about what I can accomplish. I'm on target for not only meeting my goals but exceeding them...But, apparently, he doesn't hear what I'm saying, or he's not convinced so he starts to tell me how I should run the project...I'm thinking he doesn't like the way I'm running the project...I object...politely. But he proceeds to tell me in great detail exactly about these changes I should make...

Do you know there are people in this world that actually like being told what to do?

What do you bet that I'm one of them?

HMHPs don't like being told what to do. So, what do you think my reaction was? Let me give you one clue...I used to be very emotional—or let's just say outspoken.

I don't think he expected me to say anything. Back then, well, it was very easy for me to lose my cool. I was very defensive and yes you could even say uncooperative. So I'll leave the rest of the conversation to your imagination.

What really surprised me, he invited me to breakfast again...

and again. Each time the same thing happened...he would examine my project, ask for a blow-by-blow description of what I was doing and then he'd give me a blow-by-blow description of his step-by-step approach. He is a very smart man, but there were no options; he told me exactly how to run my projects and how to deal with the people, even though I had other ideas.

Despite our disagreements, we were successful—my boss, me, the projects I worked on, the company. In fact, I was told consistently how incredible my accomplishments were. But there was always a tension between us, my boss and me.

Well, I kept my resume in the top drawer of my desk all that year. How many of you have done that? You can't bring yourself to leave in the middle of a project. All the while you're working you have one foot out the door; you're looking for something else, something more rewarding. Well, when I was done with my project, I was on my way to something else and something much bigger.

It was one year from the time I started that job to the time I left. I took what I had learned and moved on to the next job. The next job was in the same industry. I took what I learned and moved on. Each job I went to, I was successful...each job I went to was a promotion.

With every move, I was more and more successful, I made more money, had more responsibility, a better title...but all the time what I felt was misunderstood. What was really wrong, what I've learned since then, is there is a better way to manage people like me. For the companies I worked for, all of that learning and all of the ideas I had for moving my projects forward faster, more profitably were lost. They were lost the minute I walked out the door. A huge gush of wind as I slammed the door behind me and a breath of fresh air as I moved to something new.

That's what a high-maintenance employee is all about. When I wasn't given the freedom to run my own projects...I was just frustrated. Even though I was successful, it just wasn't rewarding. So I moved on looking for something more challenging. Trying to figure out why I had such a difficult time finding where I fit. Why my bosses found me so high maintenance.

3. Availability of new opportunities and challenges

High-maintenance employees are driven people. Put them in charge of a new project or give them the task of creating one. Make sure that you have another new project waiting for them once their current project ends. This will continue to fuel them and prevent boredom from setting in.

4. Opportunity to advance

High-maintenance employees thrive on growth opportunities and look for jobs where they can continually advance their position. These individuals get bored easily, so it is important to create a plan for them to continually move forward in their careers. Identify the talents, skills, and interests of your high-maintenance employees. Discuss with them the experience, the behaviors, and the results they need to help them grow within your department or organization. Then create jobs and career paths that keep them challenged.

5. Creative freedom

Give your high-maintenance employees creative freedom. They are motivated by developing the big-picture idea. They tend to think in broader views and will serve you and your organization best if they are driving and executing their plan. Don't restrict them. Give them the flexibility and freedom to innovate.

6. Recognition of achievements and contributions

High-maintenance employees enjoy being told that they have done exceptional work. They like to feel as though they are leading the pack through their own accomplishments. This is in part due to their ego drive and in part because of their competitive nature. Make employee recognition a strong part of your company culture.

7. A feeling of adding value

Your high-maintenance employees will feel valued if you make sure they have exciting work to do. High-maintenance employees want to feel a sense of accomplishment—a sense that they're really contributing. Set growth plans for your high-maintenance employees that provide them with new challenges, chances to learn new skills, and opportunities to lead. This is a sure-fire way to make your high-maintenance employees feel they are valued members of your organization.

High-maintenance employees simply don't leave jobs where they feel challenged, have exciting work to do, are rewarded appropriately, and feel their contributions matter.

Understanding how to motivate and reward high-maintenance employees is such an important aspect of managing them that the next chapter is devoted to those topics.

Moving Forward

Creating the right environment is essential to overcoming the natural tendency of HMHPs to become bored easily and to switch jobs frequently. Given an exciting, fun, challenging environment in which they can excel, HMHPs will be more content and less tempted to jump ship. Focusing significant time and effort on understanding and building the environment that HMHPs prefer is an essential leadership task.

Your current high-maintenance employees can play a key role in helping newly hired HMHPs adapt to your organization. By assigning them the role of mentor, you can also add an interesting component of leadership to their jobs that will reinforce their own desire to stay with your company.

Make a special effort to get to know your HMHPs and what motivates them and makes them tick. Then create an environment that leverages this knowledge and helps make sure your superstars stay around a while.

CHAPTER 5

A Coaching Strategy for Leading and Managing Your High-Maintenance Employees

"A coach is someone who tells you what you don't want to hear, who has you see what you don't want to see, so you can be who you have always known you could be."

—Tom Landry, former head coach, Dallas Cowboys

This chapter covers:
- The importance of using a questioning leadership style as opposed to a directive style when coaching high-maintenance employees
- How coaching your high-maintenance employees differs from coaching other behavioral styles
- Detailed coaching strategies for managing high-maintenance employees
- Ways to adapt your leadership communication style so that it's effective with high-maintenance employees and non-high-maintenance employees

During a conference, Jim Collins, author of *Good to Great*, talked about some of the qualities of the great leaders who were defined in his book. Many of the great leaders, he said, had law degrees. As a lawyer himself, he went on to say that he thought the reason for this is that lawyers are taught to ask the questions. Leaders without this training, he said, often think they need to give the answers. Asking questions instead of giving the answers is a key ingredient to leading your high-maintenance employees.

Coaching Other Behavioral Styles

Here are the communication techniques more readily accepted by the other behavioral types, the non-high-maintenance employee styles:

- Remember that these individuals may be somewhat reserved. That means they tend not to start discussions, so you want to provide more opportunities for casual discussions. You still need to present the information in a logical manner and give them enough time to ask questions. You also want to give them time to talk about their worries, their concerns, and their conflicts. You really want to do this in a low-risk, private setting. They do not to like to talk about these things in a public forum.
- Engage your non-high-maintenance employees in formal communications in a businesslike atmosphere. Avoid personal references and discussions. You want to state the purpose of the communication up front, covering the topics in a logical, systematic manner.
- Be prepared for them to aggressively question the information you're providing. Sometimes they may have difficulty storing information that conflicts with their perception of how things should be. Make sure to check for points of disagreement or misunderstanding. When you respond, present specific information in a nondefensive way. Then give them time to process the information before responding. Don't forget to set aside a time to meet later for finalizing the discussion.

The Coaching Approach

Use a coaching approach, based on questioning rather than informing, for leading high-maintenance employees. This will stop you from taking away the creative problem-solving aspects of the job that high-maintenance employees thrive on. A coaching method that encourages participation in decision making will help ensure that high-maintenance employees take ownership for the decisions and goals set.

Here are basic guidelines for communicating when coaching your high-maintenance employees:

Get to the point.

While using the questioning approach, it is still important to be direct without spending a lot of time on chitchat.

Always state where you agree, so state the areas of shared agreement before moving into areas where there is less agreement. Realize that because high-maintenance employees are optimistic by nature they are going to practice selective perception. They are only going to hear or remember information that they agree with. Check at the end of the discussion that everything was heard and understood by accurately summarizing the statements.

Keep the discussions more informal.

You want to get your high-maintenance employees involved in an informal open-ended conversation. Choose a more social environment, maybe over lunch or breakfast, where you can provide an opportunity to share stories, experiences, and ideas and respond to each other in that setting.

Provide direction to keep them on the subject.

Whenever I coach someone who is a HMHP, I always have to make an effort to keep them on the subject.

For example, we might do an exercise on performance standards. I'll say something like, "Let's talk about all of the tasks and activities that are required by the job you are hiring for. Then let's allocate the time required to accomplish each of those tasks. So when someone begins the job, they will know right away how they should be spending their time."

Often, with the HMHP it's really powerful to create a defined task, because you're always pulling them in and back to what has been defined. Once the result or goal has been defined, the HMHP will be easier to coach. You need to provide direction to keep them close to the discussion. Otherwise you'll never finish within a reasonable timeframe.

Provide Feedback.

High-maintenance employees have difficulty listening to negative information. You need to be specific about where they've made mistakes, but it's difficult to determine if they really absorbed this information. The most difficult part for you will be making sure that your high-maintenance employees acknowledge what you are telling them. They are poor listeners. Have them repeat back to you what they have heard.

Coaching Strategies

You probably know who the low-maintenance high performers in your company are already. Those are your top performers...the people who give you great work, great results, without sucking the life out of you. Below outlines the basic management strategies and preferred techniques for handling specific types of coaching with high-maintenance employee and low-maintenance high performers, such as decision-making, problem-solving, and delegating.

Decision making

People can increase their effectiveness by recognizing and valuing the decision-making styles of others. Non-high-maintenance employees approach decision making slowly and methodically while calculating the risk. Others tend to be more impulsive and are more comfortable with higher levels of risk taking. Your high-maintenance employees are risk takers.

By understanding the individual differences, you can be more flexible in your approaches to decision making. You can adapt your style to the needs of others and also the work environment.

Non-high-maintenance employees need time to think through things in a step-by-step manner. You want to support their methodical, logical approach to making higher-risk decisions, and you want to coach them on which decisions are lower risk and can be made more quickly. They may tend to procrastinate on decisions involving personal conflict. Discuss how the decision is going to improve the overall well-being and stability of the group because they tend to be very team-oriented.

Non-high-maintenance employees may approach decision making in an analytical manner. Discuss the appropriate amount of time to spend on the analysis part because they get caught up in that. And then set time limits for a decision. You want to guard against them getting bogged down in considering what-if scenarios. Then provide reassurances of what will be the personal consequences of them being wrong.

When leading high-maintenance employees, coach them on their approach to decision making by making sure they consider all the options and possible consequences. Be aware that they tend to be quick decision makers. Coach them on taking time to gather information and to consider possible consequences before making possible decisions. You want to point out the benefits of the improved results that may come from taking more time to make decisions. Coach them on using a more logical, fact-based approach rather than emotions or gut feel, which is their preferred approach.

Problem solving

Problem solving is similar to decision making in that it requires the evaluation of various plans and ideas before choosing the best way to accomplish a result.

When leading non-high-maintenance employees, support them by using a step-by-step approach to problem solving, which is their preferred style. For them, problem solving is all about relying on things that are proven, so you'll need to coach them to develop innovative approaches to problem solving. You want to allow them time to study problems before implementing solutions, and then give them direction in terms of which problems require studying and which require immediate action, because they will get caught up and bogged down in the studying part.

Use an analytical approach to solving problems. Help them understand all of the contributing factors and possible consequences. Coach them on alternate problem-solving techniques for problems that need immediate solutions. Be wary; they are cautious. They want to find the perfect solution. Help them develop a workable solution rather than a perfect one.

In working with your high-maintenance employees, the more you can work with them in a way that compliments their natural styles, the more successful the solutions will be and the greater their ownership of the process.

Take a practical results-oriented approach. Look for simple, easy ways to implement solutions and direct your high-maintenance employees toward considering the long-term consequences. Coach them in handling more complex problems slowly, to avoid rushing over something simply just to get to the results. Avoid putting them in situations that involve solving complex, detailed problems that will require a great deal of follow-up.

Be prepared to coach them towards using logical, problem-solving processes rather than relying on their gut. Expect them to have difficulty in acknowledging that the problem exists because they can be overly optimistic. Help them to see actual or potential consequences or clearly state what they may be.

Delegating

Non-high-maintenance employees need a step-by-step explanation of what's required with written documentation whenever possible. Be available for follow-up questions and clarify what resources are available for completing the assignment. They will need assistance gaining cooperation from other people when it's necessary. Give them logical, accurate, precise descriptions of performance expectations, standards, and expectations for quality.

To give this group a sense of how they fit into the big picture, always explain why the assignment's being done and how it's necessary to the overall operations. Provide an opportunity to discuss alternate ways of completing the assignment for determining what resources are available.

If you are delegating to someone who is outside of the HMHP category you may also demonstrate how the delegated assignment is helping others. Recognize and reward predictable, steady performance, and provide them with the opportunity to work cooperatively with others. They like to achieve tangible results, things that they can see, because that is motivating to them. Create opportunities for them to demonstrate their expertise and support their efforts to create quality results. Provide situations where their logical and systematic tendencies will contribute to long-term success.

When delegating to high-maintenance employees, tell them what results you need by when and let them determine how to get it done. Specify what their authority is and what the available resources are, then allow them to act independently within those limits. You must also be sure to state what those limits are. Clarify their understanding about specific performance expectations and the time frames to get it done. Establish a clear understanding of how to structure the process for completing the task, especially when dealing with more complex tasks or assignments that require them to be more methodical and more strategic.

Advising

When receiving advice, some people prefer directness, while others will prefer a more indirect approach. What's important here is that you can actually use the information about another person's behavioral style to develop more flexible approaches to advising that individual.

With non-high-maintenance employees, take time to draw out their true thoughts and feelings about the situation, and help them develop a step-by-step plan for change within a defined time limit. Provide encouragement and support for developing assertive behavior.

Reduce potential defensiveness by acknowledging areas in which they excel or are highly competent. Another way to approach non-high-maintenance employees is to state the change that is needed, to explain why the change is necessary, and then solicit the person's thoughts about the solution. Always give someone with this style the opportunity to think about the solution and develop a strategy before actually committing to a solution.

When giving advice to high-maintenance employees, you want to focus on the obstacles for achieving results and how to eliminate them. Then, present what changes are needed and request solutions from them.

Provide them with an opportunity to express and acknowledge their feelings and then redirect their attention to facts and results. Use open-ended questions like what, when, where, and how to generate specific actions for change.

Correcting

People respond better to what you say if how you say it meets their style need for receiving feedback. Some are more open to receiving corrective feedback than others. What may make one person feel defensive may be very different from what makes another person feel defensive. If you understand another person's behavior style, you can anticipate his/her responses to specific feedback. The corrective feedback is more likely to be heard in a way that leads to a positive result.

When correcting a non-high-maintenance employee, balance the statement of what improvement is necessary with recognition of areas in which the person is performing well. Then provide assistance in creating a step-by-step plan for improvement. Provide feedback on gradual improvements in performance.

Be sure to separate issues of performance from issues of the individual's worth as a person. At times, people in this group may become defensive when their performance is criticized. What tends to work best is to stick to a specific factual discussion about the current results and what performance improvement is necessary. Develop a plan for improving performance and close the discussion by agreeing what the improvement will be and by what date. And then set a date for formally reviewing progress on the plan.

I was working with one executive on this. He was concerned about a manager of his who wasn't meeting deadlines. The manager had no idea that his boss felt this way. The manager would often say, "I do all these other things, so if I miss a few deadlines over here it's not a big deal."

What my client has learned is that changing his own approach to the problem will enable the manager to correct his behavior. He focuses the manager on the priorities he wants him to work on. The boss is training the manager by consistently saying, "These are the things I am always going to ask about." The manager then comes prepared, knowing that it is not only where he's supposed to focus his time, but that he is being held accountable for those objectives. I also suggested that my client shift his focus somewhat so that he stops telling himself what role he has in managing people and instead asks his people what role he could play in enabling them to succeed. In addition, many managers make the mistake of asking versus telling. What this manager has done in order to get different results from his employee is to use a questioning approach while at the same time form new patterns and habits. He is consistent in what he asks for and how he asks in an effort to keep his employee on track and meeting deadlines.

Acknowledging

People feel most genuinely valued when they receive compliments for those personal characteristics that they consider strengths in themselves and others. A characteristic viewed as a compliment by one person, however, may be considered an insult by another. You can apply your knowledge about another person's behavioral style to use compliments that he or she is most likely to accept and appreciate.

With non-high-maintenance employees, be sincere. Tell them privately the value of their efforts at maintaining stability and producing results consistently. Use accurate statements, in private, about their competence.

When complimenting high-maintenance employees, use brief, direct statements focusing on their achievements, their results, and their leadership ability. Give them praise and recognition for their positive attitude, their verbal ability, and their interpersonal skills.

Training

People have different requirements for the amount of direction, support, and information they need to develop a new skill. When coaching non-high-maintenance employees around training issues, you want to create a step-by-step plan for development and provide one-on-one hands-on instruction. Provide written procedures whenever possible. Allow them more time to feel confident and conduct regular friendly follow-up and reassurances that they're doing the right thing. Check for understanding at key points and give them time to process the information. Let them practice new skills on their own and then be available to respond to their questions. Provide additional explanations and define time limits for developing adequate skills rather then absolute mastery.

When developing a HMHP, you want to make them productive quickly. Show them the quickest, most practical way to get to the results. Emphasize only the key details necessary to get to the results. Define the limits on their authority because they'll take over everything if left on their own. Reduce the amount of detail, as they get overwhelmed by details. Finally, give assistance for providing a structure for completing the actual task.

By applying what you've learned about behavioral styles in all aspects of your coaching, both with high-maintenance employees and others, you will significantly improve your leadership abilities. Less conflict will exist within the organization and this will lead to greater success and job satisfaction for everyone. Keep in mind the following strategies when coaching your high-maintenance and non-high-maintenance employees.

Coaching strategies for high-maintenance employees:

Decision Making
- Make sure your high-maintenance employees consider all options and possible consequences.
- Use a more logical-fact based approach.

Problem Solving
- Take a practical results-oriented approach.
- Avoid putting them in situations that involve solving complex, detailed problems that will require a great deal of follow up.

Delegating
- Tell them what results you need by when and let them determine how to get it done.

Advising
- Focus on the obstacles for achieving results and how to eliminate them.
- Use open-ended questions like what, when, where, and how to generate specific actions for change.

Correcting
- Be firm and direct, stating the desired result a well as the

current level of performance.

- Direct the discussion to what actions that person is going to take to improve performance and avoid extensive discussions about other people and other situations.
- End your discussion with a commitment to a specific result to be achieved within a specific time, and then focus on the positive outcomes of improving performance and how the person will look good in the eyes of others.

Acknowledging

- Use brief, direct statements focusing on their achievements, their results, and their leadership ability.
- Give them praise and recognition for their positive attitude, their verbal ability, and their interpersonal skills.

Training

- Make them productive quickly.
- Show them the quickest, most practical way to get to the results.

Coaching strategies for non-high-maintenance employees:

Decision Making

- Set timelines.
- Provide reassurances that they are approaching the problem correctly.

Problem Solving

- Support them by using a step-by-step approach to problem solving.
- Coach them to develop innovative approaches to problem solving and give them time to study problems before implementing solutions. Be specific on which problems require studying and which require immediate action.

Delegating

- Give them logical, accurate, precise descriptions of performance expectations, standards, and expectations for quality.
- Be available for follow-up questions and clarify what resources are available for completing the assignment.

Advising

- Help them create a step-by-step plan for change in a defined time limit.
- Provide encouragement and support for developing assertive behavior.

Correcting

- Balance the statement of what improvement is necessary with recognition of areas in which the person is performing well. Then provide assistance in creating a step-by-step plan for improvement.
- Provide feedback on gradual improvements in performance.

Acknowledging

- Be sincere.
- Tell them privately the value of their efforts at maintaining stability and producing results consistently.
- Use accurate statements, in private, about their competence.

Training

- Create a step-by-step plan for development
- Provide one-on-one hands-on instruction.
- Provide written procedures whenever possible.

Moving Forward

Remember, as a leader, to leverage your new understanding of behavioral styles to coach your HMHPs in ways that align with their communication preferences. You can help them improve their performance in decision making and problem solving, and delegating work to others by matching your coaching style to their behavioral style.

Also, when advising, correcting, acknowledging, and training your HMHPs, make sure you do so in a way that fits their behavioral style. Your non-HMHPs can also benefit by having coaching that is done in a manner that fits their preferred communication style.

In the next chapter, we'll look at how to successfully integrate high-maintenance employees into a team.

CHAPTER 6

Integrating High-Maintenance Employees into Your Team

"Individual commitment to a group effort—that is what makes a team work, a company work, a society work, a civilization work."

—Vince Lombardi

In this chapter, you'll learn:
- What it really means to be a team
- How to structure your team to make the most of the skills of high-maintenance employees
- Pitfalls to watch out for when high-maintenance employees are part of your team

About 60 percent of the leaders I coach ask, "How do I manage my high-maintenance employees so they operate as part of my team?" Helping their high-maintenance employees to work as part of a team and dealing with the consequences if they don't is one of the greatest challenges managers face.

High-maintenance employees prefer to work independently. Because they prefer to work alone, they are less likely to share their experiences and their knowledge with the team or the organization, which also results in this resource being under-utilized. Often they don't follow the rules, which makes it difficult for you to reinforce the structure for the rest of the team.

You can use your understanding of the behaviors, preferred communication style, and preferred operating environment of high-maintenance employees to help integrate them into the team environment. The primary characteristics you can use to drive high-maintenance employees to operate within the team structure include their:

- Innovative and creative tendencies
- Desire to achieve results
- Appreciation for learning new skills
- Need for recognition
- Image awareness
- Drive for working efficiently

Integrating high-maintenance employees into a team is challenging. Understanding their characteristics and the effects that they can have on a team is important. What is equally important is to understand the overall characteristics of a team.

While understanding how the characteristics of high-maintenance employees affect their interaction in the team setting is important, it is equally important to understand the characteristics of a team.

Understanding the Team Concept

For years now, we've all heard and become familiar with the term "teamwork." So much so, in fact, that it seems overused, outdated, and even indifferent. However, teamwork, contrary to popular belief, has not yet come into its own.

To incorporate your high-maintenance employees into a team, it is important to understand the difference between a team and a group.

Group: A collection of people who come together to communicate, address a challenge, or coordinate an event.

Team: A collection of people who come together to achieve a clear and compelling common objective that they have participated

Groups...	Teams...
❖ Operate by external rules of order. Individual agendas come into play and overshadow the common good. While the employee may work closely with a group of people in a specific department, that employee is not focused on team or organizational goals. They are geared toward attaining whatever benefits them most.	❖ Operate by their own set of team norms. They develop a system of order that functions to keep them focused on contributing their greatest strengths. Teams don't allow individual agendas to rule their thinking or deter them from their goals.
❖ Focus on information sharing and coordinating. While this concept may sound exceptional and productive, in all actuality it is nothing more than basic data flow. What happens once the group shares or coordinates its information? What purpose does the information serve? Who will be responsible for developing or using the information for the greater good of the organization? Usually, a rift is formed about what to do next.	❖ Focus on problem solving and process improvement. A true team will take information sharing and coordination one step further. They will extract what is needed to develop, discuss, and implement needed changes in order to effectively and collectively solve problems and improve existing processes.
❖ Have a fixed chairperson. There is normally a constant battle for power among groups. The lack of cohesion leaves each group member fighting for his/her place in the rank and file. The end result is that several employees fall under the rule of one. Yes, there may be discussions and meetings, but in the end one person—the chairperson—has the final say.	❖ Share leadership. Teams understand that each person has strengths and weaknesses. They further understand that a collective conscience is able to create more well-rounded decisions and plans of action than a dictatorship. Because of the shared leadership teams enjoy, all team members feel comfortable to express themselves which, in turn, brings a comprehensive ability to decision making.

in defining. To the members of a true team, that objective is more important than their own individual pursuits. This dimension gives the team its cohesion and is an important link to what motivates your high-maintenance employees.

The chart on the previous page outlines the primary characteristics of groups and teams and shows the differences between them. Most high-maintenance employees operate as though they are a part of a group, not a part of a team. By operating as a part of a group, they have their own agenda; they are not focused on the goals of the organization or the goals of the team. They tend to dominate or lead the group, which often results in other group members falling under their rule and following the agenda of the HMHP instead of the real agenda of the team.

A true team focuses on problem solving, and its members understand each other's strengths and weaknesses. It may have a leader. However, the team is able to create more well-rounded decisions and plans of action than a dictatorship will.

During the evolution of the teamwork concept, a fine line between "groups" and "teams" was smeared in the minds of many. It was thought that by providing all employees with a written description of mission statements and goals, each could be deemed a "team member." In fact, nothing is further from the truth. It is because of this misinterpretation that the notion of teamwork has remained an untapped goldmine and is just now actually coming into its own.

Operating as Part of a Team

As you may guess based on what you're learned so far, some of the characteristics of the team environment are difficult for high-maintenance employees to adjust to. High-maintenance employees would just as soon set the agenda by themselves. So you will have to work hard to help your high-maintenance employees integrate into your team.

Giving high-maintenance employees structure is important to ensure that they give you the outcomes you need. It is important to set up the structure from the beginning of the working relationship. But they need to view this structure as if you, their manager, are not telling them what to do.

Developing team standards

Each team should create standards to make sure they have sufficient structure for completing and reporting on their goals. Some examples of standards the team might develop include:

- Change work schedules
- Identify performance problems
- Schedule breaks and vacations
- Solicit customer feedback
- Propose training plans
- Recommend increasing staff to meet work demands

High-maintenance employees need to know what is expected of them and what the results need to be, but they don't want to have that defined for them. Let your high-maintenance employees work with you to develop those standards for the team.

Make sure that you do the following to work with your high-maintenance employees to get them to work as a part of a team:

- Be the facilitator. Your role as their manager is to be the facilitator.
- Have a separate off-line conversation with your high-maintenance employees to explore the possible structures before proposing to the team.

When you involve your high-maintenance employees in designing the standards up front, you have a greater likelihood of getting their commitment and buy-in. High-maintenance employees are creators and innovators; they're results driven, so by involving them in the creation, you have a better chance of getting the needed results.

High-maintenance employees as group leaders

It is important for the team to identify roles for individuals and assign up front how each person is going to contribute overall. As part of this structure, it will be to your advantage and the company's to ask your high-maintenance employees to lead your teams. This will help you get results. They are the drivers. Your non-high-maintenance performers tend to be the supporters.

A way to hold HMHPs accountable for leading the team is to have them report the team's progress directly to you, their manager. This helps keep them on track. Make sure you have regular communication with your high-maintenance employees. Because of their verbal communication preference, you want to make sure you know where they are in their strategy and their thinking at all times.

With a high-maintenance employee in charge, you'll need other people to take care of the people side. High-maintenance employees are not the ones who'll massage the people and make the team feel really good. That is one reason it is important that not all team members are high-maintenance employees. Let your high-maintenance employees focus on the tasks; let the non-high-maintenance employees focus on the social aspects.

You'll also need someone to handle the details. The high-maintenance employees are not going to be so concerned with all the steps; they will want the team to fill in the holes on the process piece. They are not going to get bogged down in the details of how to carry it out. They'll look for the support of the group for adding to make something better. They'll also look to the group to do the process part. That is another reason for including non-high-maintenance employees on your teams.

Finally, you need to understand what it means to assign the team-leader role to a HMHP and why it is an effective strategy for embedding them in a team. Having the leadership role is not so important to the high-maintenance employees. It is more important for them to use the role to help them accomplish their goals, and as leader of the team, the team goals.

One of the most common questions that I am asked is how to get high-maintenance employees to be a part of a team. As we said earlier, these individuals prefer to operate independently. They like to take the lead because to them it's all about getting to the outcome. The following story is a perfect example of this.

After hearing me talk about the strategy of putting a HMHP in a leadership position, one manager said to herself, "Oh, I'm going to put Andrea in charge of this contest I'm running." A couple of weeks later, that manager questioned my strategy and told me about her assignment to Andrea. I said, "Andrea's not buying into it, is she?"

"No. In fact, she has asked me if she could turn down the leadership position without getting into trouble."

The reason the HMHP reacted so negatively to a leadership position, which the manager thought would be prestigious, was because it was not tied to any result that helped move her closer to completing her work goals.

Operating efficiently

Once you ask high-maintenance employees to become the team leader, you need to make sure that they can operate efficiently. What resources do they need? Who outside the team will help them accomplish the results? It's all about efficiency with high-maintenance employees. Identifying the resources they need up front is important.

The tricky part comes when the high-maintenance employee comes up with a really great idea. It often means changing procedures or the way in which others in the organization operate. High-maintenance employees don't understand that most people don't thrive on change the way they do. Often their innovation requires more work on the part of everyone, not just them. Of course, they don't mind the extra work, but others might resent it.

Because they are not methodical thinkers by nature, high-maintenance employees may not think about how to take a great idea from beginning to end. They just see the end! It's important for you to help them think through those steps. Often you have to slow them down and pull them in to help them figure out what they need to do to get the results that they want. Get them to think through what it will take to get from A to Z. This will save you both time and money.

Participating in meetings

Another common standard teams establish is holding weekly meetings. What happens with high-maintenance employees when the meeting agenda doesn't pertain to them? The team tends to lose them. So it is important when setting up meetings to include on the agenda decisions that tie into the individual high-maintenance employee or team goals or that produce a decision or result that the high-maintenance employee has a stake in. This will assure that not only that the high-maintenance employee attends the meeting but also participates fully since his/her self-interest is involved. Make sure the decisions have been made and the actions or next steps have been defined. Keep things moving and always define the next steps.

Providing a learning opportunity

When the company makes a commitment to send high-maintenance employees for training, they come back feeling that they are valued. Send your high-maintenance employees to workshops, seminars, or other learning experiences where they can pick up information of value and return to the team to make individual contributions with their new knowledge.

The topic has to be something that your HMHP is interested in to begin with. I'm very theoretical so learning is very important to me. As a HMHP, even as a sales manager when time was the most valuable resource I had, I loved to go to training or workshops that would help me run a better sales meetings or in some way better my performance on the job. Whatever would help me do better at my job or anything that tied into the end result motivated me.

While this might not be true for all high-maintenance employees, for the most part they want to see a return on their investment of their time, money, and their resources. So if they are going to spend their time in an experience where they can gain more knowledge on something, it has to be something that is really important to them and knowledge that they're going to use to accomplish whatever results they need to accomplish.

When they return, you need to help your high-maintenance employees disseminate the information and coach them to use it at the right time and the right place to benefit other team members. When your high-maintenance employees use the information they learn and bring it back to the team, it makes them feel a part of the team because it engages them. Integrating them into the team is all about getting them engaged and getting them committed.

For most high-maintenance employees, achievement is important. Certainly in some instances it can be the money, but their success, what they can achieve, and how the results are tied into that are really key. So bringing back this piece of information or strategy or tactic or a new way of doing things will help them and the team.

Rewarding your high-maintenance employees

For some high-maintenance employees, rather than the role of team leader, you can make them an expert in a specific area. Ask them to bring that knowledge to the team and to serve as a resource for the team. Reward them for any results that are achieved on behalf of the team from the knowledge that they bring.

Because image is important to your high-maintenance employees, it's important that they feel not only do their contributions matter, but that they also have something unique that they bring to the team.

Make sure your high-maintenance employees know where they are making a difference and that you're paying attention to them.

Once your high-maintenance employees are equipped with the skills they need to function within a team and have their minds opened to the understanding of successful team performance, they can experience higher levels of job satisfaction and increased rates of productivity.

Moving Forward

Follow these steps to smoothly integrate your HMHPs into a team:
- Put your HMHPs in charge of a team.
- Provide the team and its leader support so they can operate efficiently.
- Schedule regular reviews where they can report the team's progress directly to their manager.
- Give your HMHPs learning experiences to develop areas of expertise they can bring back and share with the group.
- Assign team roles so others on the team fill the social and process roles.
- Provide recognition for HMHPs' contributions to the team.

CHAPTER 7

Hiring High-Maintenance Employees

"Unless you're the lead dog in the pack, the view never changes."
—Warren Claxton

This chapter discusses:
- How to recognize a high-maintenance employee by looking at a resume
- Steps in the hiring process to help you manage your high-maintenance employees
- Interviewing questions that you can use to identify high-maintenance employees

One of my clients was interested in hiring a young woman highly recommended but right out of college. Prior to hiring this person the manager said, "Kathi, we've never even considered hiring a novice." The applicant completed a screening profile, including a behavioral assessment. It told us that she has tenacity, courage, and confidence. In short, she has all of the characteristics of a HMHP. Fortunately, this manager understood how to work effectively with HMHPs and didn't hesitate to hire this outstanding young woman.

Since coming on board, this seller has demonstrated her ability by getting in to see top decision makers at major businesses all over the country. She has shown more drive and potential than any other brand-new salesperson that her manager has ever met.

Spotting the Resume of a Potential High-Maintenance Employee

Even without the behavioral profile, this manager would have been able to identify his job candidate as high maintenance by carefully reviewing her résumé. Typical signs to help you identify the resumes of high-maintenance performers include:

They've been promoted.

They may have been with the same company for a long period of time, but they haven't stayed in any one position for very long. They get promoted usually within a one- to two-year period of time. If they leave a company, it's generally a step up. They leave only for a better opportunity that involves more responsibility, power, and status. HMHPs tend not to accept a lateral position, only a position that will take them to the next level. For example, if you have the résumé of someone who was a project director, then left to become a manager, and then left for a VP position, you may well be looking at the resume of a HMHP.

They've held leadership positions.

Even if they work within a team, they tend to assume a leadership position or play some sort of leadership role in most of the jobs they've had. This includes those HMHPs who have not been in the workforce for a long period of time.

They've had a lot of jobs.

Don't be surprised or dismayed by the number of jobs or positions that a HMHP has had. High-maintenance performers tend not to stay in any one place for very long because they get bored. Expect to see that they have held many positions in one organization. Often they are promoted to the next level or division to experience something new and challenging.

They emphasize goal achievement.

High-maintenance performers tend to focus their resumes on the goals they've achieved. For example, the resume might include: reached the goal of X, this was the goal of our department; our organization had a goal of X and here is how I contributed to that goal. This will also be demonstrated in their willingness to do "whatever it takes" to get things done.

They're involved in many activities.

If a résumé shows that someone is involved in lots of activities and has accomplishments outside the workplace, this individual is likely to be a high-maintenance performer. High performers juggle a lot of balls. They need to be in constant motion. They are usually taking classes or participating in activities to help them climb the next latter or accomplish specific results. The high-maintenance performer will have a pattern of success from their youth through present day which can be seen in their accomplishments.

While not all of these indicators may be present on every high-maintenance performer's resume, if you find many of these things present, then you're almost certainly looking at a candidate who fits this category.

Hiring Process for Identifying High-maintenance Performers

As I emphasized earlier, HMHPs can help drive your organization to new heights. But at the same time, there is a downside if you are unable to create the corporate culture in which these high achievers will thrive. It can be challenging and costly to recruit HMHPs who become dissatisfied and quickly move on.

This can happen when you look only at the technical skills to make hiring decisions rather than considering the values, behaviors, and attributes of the candidate as well. A hiring method that focuses only on technical skills creates a revolving door for HMHPs.

Now, we'll explore the seven steps to finding and hiring high-maintenance performers.

Step 1: Benchmark the job
Step 2: Create a well-defined job description
Step 3: Screen
Step 4: Match candidates to the benchmark
Step 5: Check references
Step 6: Profile your top candidates
Step 7: Hire your top candidate

Step 1: Benchmark the Job

Normally, when we're hiring, what do we do? We benchmark people. That is, we look at the metrics we think of for people in the position: job experience, college degrees and majors, and so forth.

But what we should be doing is benchmarking the job, not the person in that job. How do we do that? We need to determine how the job should be performed. This should not be a quick, off-the-top-of-your-head job description, but a detailed plan for the job. Benchmarking the job will set a higher standard than benchmarking your team of current performers, if your current team does not perform at a high level. Having higher standards makes it easier to create a development plan for everyone. Everyone needs continuous improvement and goals as we work to achieve maximum performance.

Commitment and accountability are key ingredients to meeting and exceeding any company's revenue goals. When the job requirements are identified, your HMHPs can be compared against a standard. After the comparison, they can be asked to commit to improve in very specific areas. You will find that when HMHPs have committed to improving, holding them accountable is easy. So before you get started, take time to benchmark the job first. Here is how you do that.

Step 2: Create a Well-Defined Job Description

Defining the job for the position you are hiring for is nothing more than documenting a concise job description that states the responsibilities, the activities, and the tasks to be performed. The purpose is to provide a thorough understanding of the job to be analyzed.

One mistake many managers make is not rewriting a job description for each job they're hiring for. For example, let's say you're hiring for several sales positions at different levels. Instead of using one generic sales position job description, you should write different ones for each level, from entry level to midlevel to senior level. While many of the things you're seeking in a sales person will be the same at each level, other things will differ, so you need separate job descriptions that lay out those differences.

Interview people who have done the job.

Ask the people who have performed a job for their input about what should be included in the job description as well as what skills a top performer would have. Once you've defined the activities and tasks for a job, you will have a better idea of what outcomes you'd like to see a person achieve by doing the job.

Define the performance standards.

A performance standard is a concise statement that defines a specific and measurable outcome that the job must achieve for the organization in order to deliver superior performance. A performance standard must be measurable. The employee shouldn't be held accountable for anything that doesn't have a definite measure. So the way to define a performance standard is to decide how many hours per week each performance standard demands and then evaluate the time required for each performance standard until the total reaches 80 percent of a normal work week. So if you have a forty-hour work week (although a HMHP would never work just forty hours), we take 80 percent, which is thirty-two hours. This leaves time for unexpected priorities driven from outside the job itself. Once you define the performance standards, prioritize them.

Let's look at a performance standard for a sales position: new business development. That's a number-one priority and it will require a sales person's focus for fifteen hours a week. Then look at another performance standard: servicing an existing customer. That priority is a number two and it will require a focus of five hours a week. The next priority is writing presentations. That will probably take five hours a week. Continue until your total equals thirty-two hours.

Create a chart to define your performance standards for each

PERFORMANCE STANDARD:	PRIORITY:	HOURS REQUIRED PER WEEK:
1. Service customers	1	6
2. New business sales calls	2	10
3. Return phone calls and emails	4	7
4. Paperwork	5	2
5. Writing proposals	3	4
6. Internal meetings	6	3
Total hours for the week:		32

position in your department or organization. It also helps new hires understand how they should allocate their time and efforts in order to be successful.

Define the characteristics of the successful performer.

A benchmarking tool helps you to define the core characteristics that you are looking for in each position that you need to hire. It provides you with a methodology for determining, for example, the behaviors needed for superior performance in the specific job. There are several benchmarking tools on the market. The tool I use includes defining the behaviors, values, and attributes required for the position.

I recommend that the hiring managers create and participate in the benchmark. After that is done, you may want to profile the top performers in the company and see how they compare against the benchmark.

In order to create a clear expectation for the level of performance required to perform in the job, you can compare the achievement level for the top and bottom performers currently in the job. This is optional, because as mentioned earlier if your current performers in the job are only giving you a C-grade performance and you use that group as a benchmark, then the benchmark for high performers will not be accurate.

Step 3: Screen

With a clearly defined job description and ways to screen resumes for hiring the HMHP, you are ready to begin screening and hiring. By holding a telephone interview you can refine your list of candidates and screen them before scheduling face-to-face interviews.

Once you have narrowed your candidates to those you feel are the best match to your position, then you're ready for the face-to-face interview. Asking the right questions is the first step to hiring the right candidate.

This section provides an extensive list of interview questions specifically targeted to elicit responses you would want to hear for hiring a HMHP. Use some of these questions for your telephone screening and then others for the face-to-face interview.

When you interview your potential HMHP job candidates, it's important to use specific interview questions that will give you insight into the candidates' core competencies, behaviors, and values. Here is a guide of interviewing questions that will help you identify

FCO|Footnote Reference|FCC| TriMetrix™ – Copyright |FCO|emailstyle192003 Bill J. Bonnstetter and William T. Brooks|FCC|

whether a job candidate has the characteristics of a HMHP. Also included are follow-up questions that you can use based on the candidate's answers to your initial question, as well as responses that you could expect to hear coming from a HMHP. Generally two questions with appropriate follow-up questions per category are sufficient for matching your candidates to the job.

Competency questions

The following competency questions are specifically designed to elicit responses that will help you determine whether your candidates are HMHPs. Choose the questions that reflect competencies included in your job description.

Self-direction

Being self-directed is the ability to prioritize and complete tasks in order to deliver desired outcomes within allotted time frames. Questions you should ask to get at this quality are:

- Can you tell me about an experience you've had managing a new project?
- What kind of a process did you follow?
- How did you keep everything on schedule?
- What did you do when something didn't go as planned?
- Can you tell me what was most successful about your project?
- What were your greatest challenges?
- What did you learn from them?
- What did you do differently the next time?

Your goal is to determine their desire to get to the result, as well as their ability to achieve or surpass set goals. Consider asking this question and its follow-up:

- Has there ever been a time when you've had too much to accomplish within the time allotted?
- What did you do about it?

If you're dealing with high-maintenance performers, they will tell you that they have put in a lot of extra time. They tend to put in a lot of extra time if that's what they feel will help them get to the goal.

They have a high sense of urgency to get the job done.

To gauge efficiency, ask these or similar questions:

- What method do you use for planning how you get your work done?
- How much do you accomplish in a day compared to others you work with and why?

HMHPs will tend to answer this by telling you that they operate efficiently and at high levels of productivity. They will talk about the outcome and achievements, but not necessarily how they got there.

Recovering from adversity

Another core attribute for HMHPs is resiliency, the ability to quickly recover from adversity. HMHPs tend not to take feedback well; they don't like to be criticized. Their focus on the task(s) at hand allows them to move more quickly than the average person, so it unfortunately follows that they sometimes don't notice that other people are getting frustrated because they are plowing right ahead.

Here are questions and answers about their ability to recover quickly from adversity:

- Tell me about a problem, controversy, or difference of opinion you've had with a boss or coworker that interfered with how you were doing something.
- How did you evaluate their position and whether it was warranted?
- How did you resolve it?
- Did you change your opinion or your approach based on their feedback?

HMHPs want to be right, so they have a strong conviction as to why things happen the way they do. They are not very accepting when things aren't right. So look for signs. They tend to be much harder on themselves than they are on anyone else. It is this self-actualization and self-realization that forces them to get things right and not be wrong.

One of the things you will be looking for to identify HMHPs is not only whether they moved quickly, but whether they came up with another solution to solve the problem. They like to know that they have options. They like to solve the pieces of the puzzle and they like to do it quickly. If they can't solve it quickly, then they're going to move on to something else. So talk to them about how long it took them to move onto something else. Did they solve this puzzle?

Even though they don't take criticism very well, they're going to want to fix something. You're looking for action. And they will tell you that they did it and they did it quickly. Their self-image is important, so they're not going to want to be perceived as lacking in any area. It may or may not have stuck, but they usually learn something valuable and they are so hard on themselves that they usually take that to heart.

Results orientation

Results orientation is the ability to identify actions necessary to complete tasks and obtain results. Ask this question:

- Give me examples of some of the goals you've set and completed.

HMHPs will tell you they have had several goals that they work on at one time. They like to talk about what they have accomplished. This is easy for them to do because they usually have a long list. Here are some other questions you can ask to determine HMHP results orientation:

- Given the choice, would you prefer managing one long complex project or multiple short projects, and why?
- Tell me about the longest project you've worked on and how long it took to complete.
- What did you like most and least about it?
- What was easiest and most difficult about it?

High-maintenance performers typically finish things that they start. They want completion. They start few things that they don't complete. They like a challenge; so look for the risks that they took, the challenges they have overcome, and those things that aren't average risks. Sometimes they have to go back and start over, because they didn't fully think through their course of action, their plan, or didn't consider the consequences of each action. So they can get almost to the end of a project and have to begin again. A high-maintenance performer will tell you that they have many projects that they are working on at any given time.

It's not unusual to see a high-maintenance performer leave a job before they have another one because they had a conviction about something. Don't be surprised. They tend to be not very easily forgiving when someone doesn't do what they say they're going to do.

Another question about results that you can ask is:

- Has anyone ever failed to meet a commitment to you? If so, how did you handle it?

Nine times out of ten the high-maintenance performer will write that person off. The most difficult project for HMHPs is one that involves depending on other people, because they prefer to work alone and not depend on others. This person will demonstrate real drive. The high-maintenance performer is aggressive or dominant, which will be evident in their need for closure and meeting their commitments. Their behavior is reflected in their impatience and their willingness to "do what it takes" to get things done.

Behavioral questions

Behaviors, as we've defined before, are the natural tendencies individuals have, their communications style, and their preferred method of operating. The following questions will help you determine whether your candidates have the positive qualities of a HMHP.

Acceptance of change

HMHPs like frequent change, so you want to hire a HMHP into a job that requires lots of activity or change. Ask these questions:

- How would you respond to a request to deliver your project sooner?

• What if you were asked to change your priorities midway through a project? How would you respond then?

You want to see that the person thrives on these sorts of challenges and that they take them very seriously as they do in the work being done. HMHPs will try to solve the problem. They will not give up until they find a solution. HMHPs will feel absolutely and completely frustrated, however, if the change comes so often that they can never achieve results.

Adaptability

You want to test the respondent's level of patience and impatience. High-maintenance performers will say they are very impatient. Ask questions like this one:

• How do you react to someone who needs to discuss detail after detail and digest every proposal or idea you have?

High-maintenance performers will tell you they have a hard time working with slower-moving people and people who need a lot of detail about something, because they themselves tend to move very quickly. They tend to be opinionated and strong-willed. Here is another question to ask about their ability to cope:

• Have you been in a situation of frequent interruptions by others? How do you handle yourself in that kind of environment?

This goes back to impatience. High-maintenance performers tend not to like interruptions, because they are so task focused that they're looking only at their own tasks. They'll drop something and have a sense of urgency to handle that interruption and then move onto the next thing, or go back to what they were working on. They tend to give you what you ask for very quickly. They prefer operating independently, without a lot of structure.

Value questions

Value questions help you understand whether the values of the candidate are consistent with the hiring position. Typical values, according to Target Training International™ (TTI) in their

Personal Interests Attitudes and Values™ assessment (PIAV™), are frequently broken down into six categories: utilitarian, individualistic, theoretical, aesthetic, traditional, and social. For example, if the candidate is looking for high-income potential and the position provides little or no incentive pay for high performance, there is a mismatch. If the candidate values personal relationships and is looking for a position with a great deal of human interaction but the job requires working independently in isolation, there is a mismatch. We will take a close look at two values that signify high-maintenance performers.

Utilitarian value

The utilitarian value is about return on investment. Oftentimes we do see that high-maintenance performers like a return on investment, whether it is one of time, money, or resources. When asked if making a lot of money is important, the answer will be "Very."

When asked, "How much money is a lot to you?" the answer will be, "As much as I can possibly make!"

Another way to get at the utilitarian value is to ask questions along this line:

• To prove your worth to management would you spend your time convincing them of what you could accomplish with a larger budget, or deliver more than expected with the budget you have?

The high-maintenance performer will talk to the bottom line and over-achieving their goals.

Individualistic

Another value that is very important and often signifies a high-maintenance performer is being individualistic. This is about leading in order to advance in one's position, while helping others to advance in their positions as well. Here are sample questions:

• How important for your job satisfaction is having decision-making authority?
• How important is it for you to be in charge of a project or situation?

HMHPs will tell you that's number one because they would prefer to do things according to how they see it should be done. They are not comfortable following the lead of others.

- Which appeals to you more: being self-directed or taking direction from others?

HMHPs don't like to take direction from others. In interview situations they might say that they are fine with taking direction, but they will ultimately confess that they are at their best when they are allowed to figure out that direction for themselves.

Step 4: Match Candidates to the Benchmark

Once you have screened and interviewed those you consider to be your top candidates, you should compare them against the benchmark that you have completed defining your ideal profile. Your ideal profile defines the behaviors, values, and attributes for superior performance in the job.

Step 5: Check References

Identifying HMHPs through a resume and a thorough interview is only part of the total selection process. There are many other factors that you need to consider in planning for this hire. Potential HMHP employees should be judged also on their hard and technical skills, specific industry knowledge, and experience. They should also undergo reference checks.

References for the high-maintenance performer will often indicate that this person was incredible at the job but not easy to work with. You might ask: Was this person results driven? Did they prefer to lead a project to get to the results? Did they operate outside of the team? Did you find it difficult pulling them into the team? Did you find them to be a producer but not easy to manage?

Step 6: Profile Your Top Candidates

Once you have completed the benchmark for the position, you have a tool for screening your candidates. However, finding HMHPs for your organization will require you to ask your applicants questions that are different than the kind you traditionally ask during the hiring process.

Behavioral profiling is an excellent way to measure if your candidates have the behaviors (sometimes referred to as the soft skills) to perform the job. The soft skills typically include the core competencies for the position. There are many behavioral profiling tools on the market today.

Look for a tool that has been validated by the U.S. Equal Employment Opportunity Commission and that has the data to accurately assess your candidates. Screen only your top candidates. Do not use behavioral profiling as a way to screen out candidates. Using a profiling tool as the only tool to screen candidates is prohibited in many states. After you have interviewed your candidates and you think they may be a match, the next step is to screen them using a behavioral profiling tool. In my company, we used one of the most thorough and widely accepted tools called the TriMetrix™ Personal Talent Report™.

The TriMetrix™ Personal Talent Report™ provides a summary of a person's talent to match the identical areas outlined in the TriMetrix™ Job Report™, the tool for capturing your benchmarked job. The TriMetrix™ Personal Talent Report™ within the framework of your company's overall selection and development processes, reveals why (values), how (behaviors), and what (attributes) an individual can contribute to the job. Each candidate is presented in an unbiased, clear picture that allows for better decision-making processes.

It includes three parts and combines the DISC, PIAV™, and Attribute Index™ into one report and is used as a screening tool for potential candidates.

DISC

DISC profile tells you how a person will perform in the job. It profiles their behavioral style.

PIAV™

The Personal Interests Attitudes and Values™ assessment tells you why a person behaves as he/she does. It profiles their internal motivation.

Attribute Index™

The Attribute Index™ tells us what a candidate will focus on. The Attribute Index™ is designed to provide insight into a person's behavioral strengths and weaknesses.

Here is some theory behind this instrument:

Dr. Hartman created the science of Axiology.

Axiology is the study of the core reasoning behind how people think, their thinking habits, how they value.

By mathematically applying a measurable order to this thought process we are able to make predictive statements about a person's potential for performance, actions, and behavior.

The following profiles on pages 83–136 are typical of a HMHP and are reproduced here with permission from TTI Performance Systems, Ltd.

Step 7: Hire Your Top Candidate

Once you've decided which candidate is the best match for the position, you will make an offer. HMHPs will want to feel in control of their destiny as soon as possible when they start. The work you've done describing the position and responsibilities will help speed the progress.

Creating an employee development plan within the first thirty

|FCO|Footnote Reference|FCC| *Attribute Index™— Copyright Innermetrix and RS Hartman Institute™*

|FCO|Footnote Reference|FCC| *Copyright Target Training International™*

days will create an even stronger commitment for HMHPs to understand their attributes and what they need to work on to be successful in the workplace. The sample employee development plan at the end of this chapter is designed to work with the behavior profiling done in Step 6. Having the profile information makes it possible to identify areas of strength and areas to improve upon for the HMHP. It will immediately give them goals to work toward and help avoid pitfalls early in their employment.

Moving Forward

Using a hiring process that includes resume screening and interview questions that elicit the core competencies, behaviors, and values of a high-maintenance performer will help you hire the right person for the job. Having a carefully developed job description that benchmarks the job with performance standards and both the hard and soft skills required to perform the job will make many areas of hiring and managing easier. For example, it will be easier for the:

- Manager to match your high-maintenance performer candidates with the right jobs
- Candidate to understand what is expected
- New hire to start performing in the job quickly
- Manager to create development plans to help employees grow and succeed in their jobs

TriMetrix™ System

Personal Talent Report

Copyright 2003, Bill Brooks and Bill J. Bonnstetter, reprinted with permission

John Doe
Sales Representative
ABC Company
10-10-2003

XB Coaching, Inc.
401-682-2859
support@xbcoaching.com

INTRODUCTION

Where Talent Meets Opportunity™

Research has proven that job-related talents are directly related to job satisfaction and personal performance. People are well positioned to achieve success when they are engaged in work suited to their inherent attributes, behavioral style, and unique values. Your TriMetrix System Personal Talent Report can be compared with specific job requirements outlined in TriMetrix System Job and Job Plus Reports. When the talent required by the job is clearly defined and in turn matched to the individual, everyone wins!

The following is a highly personalized portrait of your talent in three main sections:

SECTION 1: PERSONAL ATTRIBUTES HIERARCHY (23 AREAS)

This section presents twenty-three key personal attributes and ranks them from top to bottom, defining your major strengths. The attributes at the top highlight well-developed capabilities and reveal where you are naturally most effective in focusing your time.

SECTION 2: PERSONAL INTERESTS, ATTITUDES, AND VALUES (6 AREAS)

This section identifies what motivates you. In order to be successful and energized on the job, it is important that your underlying values are satisfied through the nature of your work. When they are, you feel personally rewarded by your work.

SECTION 3: BEHAVIORAL HIERARCHY (8 AREAS)

This section ranks the traits that most closely describe your natural behavior. When your job requires the use of your top behavioral traits, your potential for success increases, as do your levels of personal and professional satisfaction.

PERSONAL ATTRIBUTES HIERARCHY

Your unique hierarchy of personal attributes is key to your success. Knowing what they are is essential to reaching your goals. The graphs below rank your personal attributes from top to bottom.

1. DEVELOPING OTHERS: The ability to contribute to the growth and development of others.

   0....1....2....3....4....5....6....7....8....9....10
   9.6

2. EMPATHETIC OUTLOOK: The capacity to perceive and understand the feelings and attitudes of others.

   0....1....2....3....4....5....6....7....8....9....10
   9.5

3. LEADING OTHERS: The ability to organize and motivate people to accomplish goals while creating a sense of order and direction.

   0....1....2....3....4....5....6....7....8....9....10
   9.0

4. INFLUENCING OTHERS: The ability to personally affect others' actions, decisions, opinions, and thinking.

   0....1....2....3....4....5....6....7....8....9....10
   8.9

5. TEAMWORK: The ability to cooperate with others to meet objectives.

   0....1....2....3....4....5....6....7....8....9....10
   8.8

6. CONFLICT MANAGEMENT: The ability to resolve different points of view constructively.

   0....1....2....3....4....5....6....7....8....9....10
   8.6

7. CONTINUOUS LEARNING: The ability to take personal responsibility and action toward learning and implementing new ideas, methods, and technologies.

   0....1....2....3....4....5....6....7....8....9....10
   8.5

PERSONAL ATTRIBUTES HIERARCHY

8. **SELF-MANAGEMENT:** The ability to prioritize and complete tasks in order to deliver desired outcomes within allotted time frames.

0....1....2....3....4....5....6....7....8....9....10

8.3

9. **FLEXIBILITY:** The ability to readily modify, respond to, and integrate change with minimal personal resistance.

0....1....2....3....4....5....6....7....8....9....10

8.3

10. **CUSTOMER FOCUS:** A commitment to customer satisfaction.

0....1....2....3....4....5....6....7....8....9....10

8.2

11. **OBJECTIVE LISTENING:** The ability to listen to many points of view without bias.

0....1....2....3....4....5....6....7....8....9....10

8.2

12. **PLANNING AND ORGANIZATION:** The ability to establish a process for activities that lead to the implementation of systems, procedures, or outcomes.

0....1....2....3....4....5....6....7....8....9....10

8.1

13. **ACCOUNTABILITY FOR OTHERS:** The ability to take responsibility for others' actions.

0....1....2....3....4....5....6....7....8....9....10

8.0

14. **GOAL ACHIEVEMENT:** The overall ability to set, pursue, and attain achievable goals, regardless of obstacles or circumstances.

0....1....2....3....4....5....6....7....8....9....10

7.8

15. **PERSONAL ACCOUNTABILITY:** A measure of the capacity to be answerable for personal actions.

0....1....2....3....4....5....6....7....8....9....10

7.7

PERSONAL ATTRIBUTES HIERARCHY

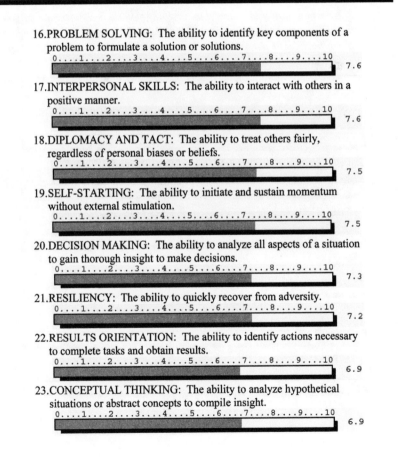

16. PROBLEM SOLVING: The ability to identify key components of a problem to formulate a solution or solutions.

0....1....2....3....4....5....6....7....8....9....10

7.6

17. INTERPERSONAL SKILLS: The ability to interact with others in a positive manner.

0....1....2....3....4....5....6....7....8....9....10

7.6

18. DIPLOMACY AND TACT: The ability to treat others fairly, regardless of personal biases or beliefs.

0....1....2....3....4....5....6....7....8....9....10

7.5

19. SELF-STARTING: The ability to initiate and sustain momentum without external stimulation.

0....1....2....3....4....5....6....7....8....9....10

7.5

20. DECISION MAKING: The ability to analyze all aspects of a situation to gain thorough insight to make decisions.

0....1....2....3....4....5....6....7....8....9....10

7.3

21. RESILIENCY: The ability to quickly recover from adversity.

0....1....2....3....4....5....6....7....8....9....10

7.2

22. RESULTS ORIENTATION: The ability to identify actions necessary to complete tasks and obtain results.

0....1....2....3....4....5....6....7....8....9....10

6.9

23. CONCEPTUAL THINKING: The ability to analyze hypothetical situations or abstract concepts to compile insight.

0....1....2....3....4....5....6....7....8....9....10

6.9

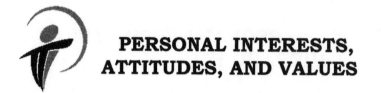

PERSONAL INTERESTS, ATTITUDES, AND VALUES

Your motivation to succeed in anything you do is determined by your underlying values. You will feel energized and successful at work when your job supports your personal values. They are listed below from the highest to the lowest.

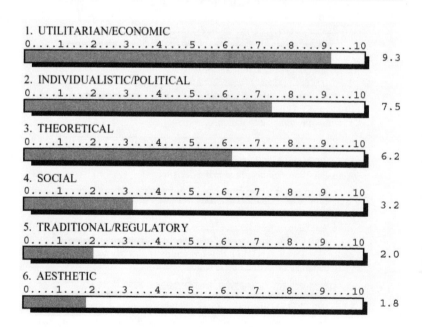

1. UTILITARIAN/ECONOMIC

0....1....2....3....4....5....6....7....8....9....10   9.3

2. INDIVIDUALISTIC/POLITICAL

0....1....2....3....4....5....6....7....8....9....10   7.5

3. THEORETICAL

0....1....2....3....4....5....6....7....8....9....10   6.2

4. SOCIAL

0....1....2....3....4....5....6....7....8....9....10   3.2

5. TRADITIONAL/REGULATORY

0....1....2....3....4....5....6....7....8....9....10   2.0

6. AESTHETIC

0....1....2....3....4....5....6....7....8....9....10   1.8

BEHAVIORAL HIERARCHY

Your observable behavior and related emotions contribute to your success on the job. When matched to the job, they play a large role in enhancing your performance. The list below ranks your behavioral traits from the strongest to the weakest.

1. COMPETITIVENESS
0....1....2....3....4....5....6....7....8....9....10
10.0

2. FREQUENT INTERACTION WITH OTHERS
0....1....2....3....4....5....6....7....8....9....10
9.0

3. FREQUENT CHANGE
0....1....2....3....4....5....6....7....8....9....10
9.0

4. CUSTOMER ORIENTED
0....1....2....3....4....5....6....7....8....9....10
8.0

5. URGENCY
0....1....2....3....4....5....6....7....8....9....10
7.5

6. VERSATILITY
0....1....2....3....4....5....6....7....8....9....10
7.5

7. ANALYSIS OF DATA
0....1....2....3....4....5....6....7....8....9....10
2.0

8. ORGANIZED WORKPLACE
0....1....2....3....4....5....6....7....8....9....10
1.0

CLARITY AND FOCUS

For consulting and coaching

CLARITY: The degree to which one can discern patterns, order, and relationships related to specific dimensions.

FOCUS: The degree to which one maintains targeted attention toward a specific factor or set of factors.

John Doe

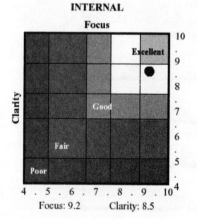

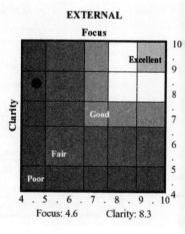

TriMetrix™-DIMENSIONAL BALANCE

For consulting and coaching

EXTERNAL FACTORS (Part 1)

* Intrinsic Dimension

    Empathetic Outlook   9.5

How do you value others?

    Understanding Attitude
    Personal Relationships
    Human Awareness
    Relating to Others

* Extrinsic Dimension

    Practical Thinking   8.6

How practically do you see the world?

    Concrete Organization

* Systemic Dimension

    Systems Judgment   6.9

How do you value systems and order?

    Results Orientation
    Sense of Belonging
    Conceptual Thinking

INTERNAL FACTORS (Part 2)

* Intrinsic Dimension

    Self-Esteem   8.6

How do you value yourself?

    Emotional Control
    Self-Improvement

* Extrinsic Dimension

    Role Awareness   8.1

How do you value what you do?

* Systemic Dimension

    Self Direction   8.8

What guides or drives your actions?

CATEGORY BREAKDOWN

For consulting and coaching

Accountability for Others
Conceptual Thinking

Conflict Management
•Internal Self-Control
•Correcting Others
•Problem Solving
•Sensitivity to Others

Continuous Learning
•Self-Improvement
•Personal Drive

Customer Focus
•Evaluating What Is Said
•Understanding Attitude
•Freedom from Prejudices

Decision Making
•Conceptual Thinking
•Theoretical Problem Solving
•Role Confidence
•Balanced Decision Making

Developing Others

Diplomacy and Tact
•Human Awareness
•Balanced Decision Making
•Freedom from Prejudices
•Emotional Control

Empathetic Outlook

Flexibility
•Self-Direction
•Integrative Ability
•Creativity

Goal Achievement
•Results Orientation
•Realistic Personal Goal Setting
•Project and Goal Focus
•Persistence

Influencing Others
•Empathetic Outlook
•Conveying Role Value
•Gaining Commitment
•Understanding Motivational Needs

Interpersonal Skills
•Empathetic Outlook
•Personal Relationships
•Emotional Control

Leading Others

Planning and Organizing
•Long Range Planning
•Concrete Organization
•Proactive Thinking

•Following Directions

Problem Solving

Resiliency
•Persistence
•Handling Rejection
•Initiative

Results Orientation
Self-Management
Self-Starting Ability

Teamwork
•Surrendering Control
•Relating to Others
•Sense of Belonging
•Sensitivity to Others

Title Changes:

Taking Responsibility:
Personal Accountability

Objective Listening:
Evaluating What Is Said

CORE ATTRIBUTE LIST

For consulting and coaching

- Realistic Expectations (9.8)
- Evaluating Others (9.8)
- Realistic Goal Setting for Others (9.8)
- Sensitivity to Others (9.8)
- Correcting Others (9.7)
- Freedom from Prejudices (9.6)
- Developing Others (9.6)
- Understanding Prospect's Motivations (9.6) *see Understanding Motivational Needs*
- Understanding Motivational Needs (9.6)
- Attitude toward Others (9.5)
- Human Awareness (9.5)
- Relating to Others (9.5)
- People Reading (9.5) *see Understanding Attitude*
- Understanding Attitude (9.5)
- Empathetic Outlook (9.5)
- Monitoring Others (9.5)
- Personal Relationships (9.5)
- Realistic Personal Goal Setting (9.2)
- Intuitive Decision Making (9.0)
- Surrendering Control (9.0)
- Leading Others (9.0)
- Persuading Others (9.0)
- Creativity (9.0)
- Self-Confidence (8.9)
- Self-Discipline and Sense of Duty (8.8)
- Self-Direction (8.8)
- Sense of Mission (8.8)
- Concrete Organization (8.6)
- Self-Assessment (8.6)
- Handling Stress (8.6)
- Self-Esteem (8.6)

- Respect for Property (8.6)
- Status and Recognition (8.6)
- Self-Improvement (8.6)
- Practical Thinking (8.6)
- Personal Commitment (8.5)
- Commitment to the Job (8.5) *see Personal Commitment*
- Personal Drive (8.5)
- Gaining Commitment (8.5)
- Meeting Standards (8.5)
- Initiative (8.5)

- Consistency and Reliability (8.3)
- Conveying Role Value (8.3)
- Proactive Thinking (8.3)
- Role Confidence (8.3)
- Enjoyment of the Job (8.3)
- Self-Management (8.3)
- Seeing Potential Problems (8.2)
- Accurate Listening (8.2) *see Evaluating What Is Said*
- Evaluating What Is Said (8.2)
- Project Scheduling (8.1)
- Long Range Planning (8.1)
- Material Possessions (8.1)
- Role Awareness (8.1)
- Accountability for Others (8.0)
- Internal Self Control (7.9)
- Sense of Timing (7.9)
- Attention to Detail (7.7)
- Personal Accountability (7.7)
- Quality Orientation (7.7)
- Taking Responsibility (7.7) *see Personal Accountability*

- Problem Solving (7.6)
- Emotional Control (7.6)
- Self-Starting Ability (7.5)
- Theoretical Problem Solving (7.4)
- Problem and Situation Analysis (7.4)
- Integrative Ability (7.4)
- Job Ethic (7.2)
- Persistence (7.2)
- Attitude toward Honesty (7.2)
- Conceptual Thinking (6.9)
- Results Orientation (6.9)
- Balanced Decision Making (6.9)
- Respect for Policies (6.9)
- Systems Judgment (6.9)
- Sense of Belonging (6.9)
- Goal Directedness (6.7) *see Project and Goal Focus*
- Project and Goal Focus (6.7)
- Handling Rejection (6.7)
- Following Directions (6.4)
- Problem Management (6.2)
- Using Common Sense (5.4)

MANAGING FOR SUCCESS®

Employee-Manager™ Version

Copyright © 1990–2002. Target Training International, Ltd., reprinted with permission.

John Doe

12-4-2003

INTRODUCTION

Behavioral research suggests that the most effective people are those who understand themselves, both their strengths and weaknesses, so they can develop strategies to meet the demands of their environment.

A person's behavior is a necessary and integral part of who they are. In other words, much of our behavior comes from "nature" (inherent), and much comes from "nurture" (our upbringing). It is the universal language of "how we act," or our observable human behavior.

In this report we are measuring four dimensions of normal behavior. They are:
- How you respond to problems and challenges.
- How you influence others to your point of view.
- How you respond to the pace of the environment.
- How you respond to rules and procedures set by others.

This report analyzes behavioral style; that is, a person's manner of doing things. Is the report 100 percent true? Yes, no, and maybe. We are only measuring behavior. We only report statements from areas of behavior in which tendencies are shown. To improve accuracy, feel free to make notes or edit the report regarding any statement from the report that may or may not apply, but only after checking with friends or colleagues to see if they agree.

"All people exhibit all four behavioral factors in varying degrees of intensity."

—W.M. Marston

GENERAL CHARACTERISTICS

Based on John's responses, the report has selected general statements to provide a broad understanding of his work style. These statements identify the basic natural behavior that he brings to the job. That is, if left on his own, these statements identify HOW HE WOULD CHOOSE TO DO THE JOB. Use the general characteristics to gain a better understanding of John's natural behavior.

John is forward-looking, aggressive, and competitive. His vision for results is one of his positive strengths. He wants to be viewed as self-reliant and willing to pay the price for success. He can be aggressive and direct, but still be considerate of people. Other people realize that directness is one of his great strengths. He prefers being a team player, and wants each player to contribute along with him. John wants to be seen as an individual who is totally keyed to results. He wants to get things done in a manner that is consistent with his perception of the "right way" of doing things. Under pressure, John has a tendency to actively seek opportunities which test and develop his abilities to accomplish results. He seeks his own solutions to problems. In this way, his independent nature comes into play. He is deadline conscious and becomes irritated if deadlines are delayed or missed. John is often frustrated when working with others who do not share the same sense of urgency. He has high ego strengths and may be viewed by some as egotistical.

John should realize that at times he needs to think a project through, beginning to end, before starting the project. Many people see his decisions as high-risk decisions. However, after the decision is made, he tends to work hard for a successful outcome. He is decisive and prefers to work for a decisive manager. He can experience stress if his manager does not possess similar traits. He finds it easy to share his opinions on solving work-related problems. John prefers authority equal to his responsibility. He is a good problem solver and troubleshooter, always seeking new ways to solve old problems. He has the unique ability of tackling tough problems and following them through to a satisfactory conclusion. Sometimes he may be so opinionated about a particular problem that he has difficulty letting others participate in the process.

GENERAL CHARACTERISTICS

John may sometimes mask his feelings in friendly terms. If pressured, John's true feelings may emerge. He likes people who give him options as compared to their opinions. The options may help him make decisions, and he values his own opinion over that of others! He may lose interest in what others are saying if they ramble or don't speak to the point. His active mind is already moving ahead. He likes people who present their case effectively. When they do, he can then make a quicker assessment or decision. John tends to be intolerant of people who seem ambiguous or think too slowly. He tends to influence people by being direct, friendly, and results-oriented. He should exhibit more patience and ask questions to make sure that others have understood what he has said. He may lack the patience to listen and communicate with slower acting people.

VALUE TO THE ORGANIZATION

This section of the report identifies the specific talents and behavior John brings to the job. By looking at these statements, one can identify his role in the organization. The organization can then develop a system to capitalize on his particular value and make him an integral part of the team.

- Initiates activity.

- Competitive.

- Verbalizes his feelings.

- Innovative.

- Challenge-oriented.

- Motivates others towards goals.

- Challenges the status quo.

CHECKLIST FOR COMMUNICATING

Most people are aware of and sensitive to the ways with which they prefer to be communicated. Many people find this section to be extremely accurate and important for enhanced interpersonal communication. This page provides other people with a list of things to DO when communicating with John. Read each statement and identify the three or four statements which are most important to him. We recommend highlighting the most important "DO's" and provide a listing to those who communicate with John most frequently.

Do:

- Provide questions, alternatives, and choices for making his own decisions.

- Provide testimonials from people he sees as important.

- Offer special, immediate, and continuing incentives for his willingness to take risks.

- Motivate and persuade by referring to objectives and results.

- Present the facts logically; plan your presentation efficiently.

- Ask for his opinions/ideas regarding people.

- Support the results, not the person, if you agree.

- Leave time for relating, socializing.

- Support and maintain an environment where he can be efficient.

- Read the body language—look for impatience or disapproval.

- Provide facts and figures about probability of success, or effectiveness of options.

- Use enough time to be stimulating, fun-loving, fast-moving.

DON'TS ON COMMUNICATING

This section of the report is a list of things NOT to do while communicating with John. Review each statement with John and identify those methods of communication that result in frustration or reduced performance. By sharing this information, both parties can negotiate a communication system that is mutually agreeable.

Don't:

- Talk down to him.

- Reinforce agreement with "I'm with you."

- Forget or lose things, be disorganized or messy, confuse or distract his mind from business.

- Leave decisions hanging in the air.

- Legislate or muffle—don't overcontrol the conversation.

- Direct or order.

- Be redundant.

- Let disagreement reflect on him personally.

- Waste time trying to be impersonal, judgmental, or too task-oriented.

- Take credit for his ideas.

- Ask rhetorical questions, or useless ones.

- Come with a ready-made decision, or make it for him.

COMMUNICATION TIPS

This section provides suggestions on methods which will improve John's communications with others. The tips include a brief description of typical people with whom he may interact. By adapting to the communication style desired by other people, John will become more effective in his communications with them. He may have to practice some flexibility in varying his communication style with others who may be different from himself. This flexibility and the ability to interpret the needs of others is the mark of a superior communicator.

When communicating with a person who is ambitious, forceful, decisive, strong-willed, independent, and goal-oriented:
- Be clear, specific, brief, and to the point.
- Stick to business.
- Be prepared with support material in a well-organized "package."

Factors that will create tension or dissatisfaction:
- Talking about things that are not relevant to the issue.
- Leaving loopholes or cloudy issues.
- Appearing disorganized.

When communicating with a person who is magnetic, enthusiastic, friendly, demonstrative, and political:
- Provide a warm and friendly environment.
- Don't deal with a lot of details (put them in writing).
- Ask "feeling" questions to draw their opinions or comments.

Factors that will create tension or dissatisfaction:
- Being curt, cold, or tight-lipped.
- Controlling the conversation.
- Driving on facts and figures, alternatives, abstractions.

COMMUNICATION TIPS

When communicating with a person who is patient, predictable, reliable, steady, relaxed, and modest:

- Begin with a personal comment—break the ice.
- Present your case softly, nonthreateningly.
- Ask "how?" questions to draw their opinions.

Factors that will create tension or dissatisfaction:

- Rushing headlong into business.
- Being domineering or demanding.
- Forcing them to respond quickly to your objectives.

When communicating with a person who is dependent, neat, conservative, perfectionist, careful, and compliant:

- Prepare your "case" in advance.
- Stick to business.
- Be accurate and realistic.

Factors that will create tension or dissatisfaction:

- Being giddy, casual, informal, loud.
- Pushing too hard or being unrealistic with deadlines.
- Being disorganized or messy.

IDEAL ENVIRONMENT

This section identifies the ideal work environment based on John's basic style. People with limited flexibility will find themselves uncomfortable working in any job not described in this section. People with flexibility use intelligence to modify their behavior and can be comfortable in many environments. Use this section to identify specific duties and responsibilities that John enjoys and also those that create frustration.

- Nonroutine work with challenge and opportunity.

- Evaluation based on results, not the process.

- Tasks involving motivated groups and establishing a network of contacts.

- An innovative and futuristic-oriented environment.

- Assignments with a high degree of people contacts.

- Forum to express ideas and viewpoints.

- Democratic supervisor with whom he can associate.

PERCEPTIONS

A person's behavior and feelings may be quickly telegraphed to others. This section provides additional information on John's self-perception and how, under certain conditions, others may perceive his behavior. Understanding this section will empower John to project the image that will allow him to control the situation.

"See Yourself as Others See You"

SELF-PERCEPTION

John usually sees himself as being:

Pioneering	Assertive
Competitive	Confident
Positive	Winner

OTHER'S PERCEPTION

Under moderate pressure, tension, stress, or fatigue, others may see him as being:

Demanding	Nervy
Egotistical	Aggressive

And under extreme pressure, stress, or fatigue, others may see him as being:

Abrasive	Controlling
Arbitrary	Opinionated

DESCRIPTORS

Based on John's responses, the report has marked those words that describe his personal behavior. They describe how he solves problems and meets challenges, influences people, responds to the pace of the environment, and how he responds to rules and procedures set by others.

Dominance	Influencing	Steadiness	Compliance
Demanding	Effusive	Phlegmatic	Evasive
Egocentric	Inspiring	Relaxed	Worrisome
		Resistant to	Careful
Driving	Magnetic	Change	Dependent
Ambitious	Political		Cautious
Pioneering	Enthusiastic	Nondemonstrative	Conventional
Strong-Willed	Demonstrative		Exacting
Forceful	Persuasive	Passive	Neat
Determined	Warm		
Aggressive	Convincing	Patient	Systematic
Competitive	Polished		Diplomatic
Decisive	Poised	Possessive	Accurate
Venturesome	Optimistic		Tactful
		Predictable	
Inquisitive	Trusting	Consistent	Open-Minded
Responsible	Sociable	Deliberate	Balanced Judgment
		Steady	
		Stable	
Conservative	Reflective		Firm
		Mobile	
Calculating	Factual		Independent
Cooperative	Calculating	Active	Self-Willed
Hesitant	Skeptical	Restless	Stubborn
Low-Keyed		Alert	
Unsure	Logical	Variety-Oriented	Obstinate
Undemanding	Undemonstrative	Demonstrative	
Cautious	Suspicious		Opinionated
	Matter-of-Fact		Unsystematic
Mild	Incisive	Impatient	Self-Righteous
Agreeable		Pressure-Oriented	Uninhibited
Modest	Pessimistic	Eager	Arbitrary
Peaceful	Moody	Flexible	Unbending
		Impulsive	
Unobtrusive	Critical	Impetuous	Careless with Detail
		Hypertense	

NATURAL AND ADAPTED STYLE

John's natural style of dealing with problems, people, pace of events, and procedures may not always fit what the environment needs. This section will provide valuable information related to stress and the pressure to adapt to the environment.

PROBLEMS—CHALLENGES (Natural)

John tends to deal with problems and challenges in a demanding, driving, and self-willed manner. He is individualistic in his approach and actively seeks goals. John will attack problems and likes a position with authority and work that will constantly challenge him to perform up to his ability.

PROBLEMS—CHALLENGES (Adapted)

John's response to the environment is to be strong-willed and ambitious in his problem-solving approach. He seeks to win against all obstacles.

PEOPLE—CONTACTS (Natural)

John is enthusiastic about his ability to influence others. He prefers an environment in which he has the opportunity to deal with different types of individuals. John is trusting and also wants to be trusted.

PEOPLE—CONTACTS (Adapted)

John sees no need to change his approach to influencing others to his way of thinking. He sees his natural style to be what the environment is calling for.

NATURAL AND ADAPTED STYLE

PACE—CONSISTENCY (Natural)

John is variety-oriented and demonstrates a need to get from one activity to another as quickly as possible. He usually demonstrates a pronounced sense of urgency. He is eager to initiate change if for nothing else than for change's sake.

PACE—CONSISTENCY (Adapted)

John sees his natural activity style to be just what the environment needs. What you see is what you get for activity level and consistency. Sometimes he would like the world to slow down.

PROCEDURES—CONSTRAINTS (Natural)

John is independent by nature and feels comfortable in situations where the constraints are few and far between. He will follow rules as long as he feels that the rules are his. He has a tendency to rebel from rules set by others and wants input into any constraints.

PROCEDURES—CONSTRAINTS (Adapted)

John shows little discomfort when comparing his basic (natural) style to his response to the environment (adapted) style. The difference is not significant and John sees little or no need to change his response to the environment.

ADAPTED STYLE

John sees his present work environment requiring him to exhibit the behavior listed on this page. If the following statements DO NOT sound job related, explore the reasons why he is adapting this behavior.

- Coping with rapid changes in the work arena.

- Maintaining an ever-changing, friendly, work environment.

- Optimistic, future-oriented outlook.

- Preferring people involvement over task focus.

- Making tactful decisions.

- Positive, outgoing, friendly behavior.

- Handling a variety of activities.

- Exhibiting an active and creative sense of humor.

- Obtaining results through people.

- Meeting deadlines.

- Moving quickly from one activity to another.

- Flexibility.

KEYS TO MOTIVATING

This section of the report was produced by analyzing John's wants. People are motivated by the things they want; thus wants that are satisfied no longer motivate. Review each statement produced in this section with John and highlight those that are present "wants."

John wants:

- Work assignments that provide opportunity for recognition.

- Freedom from control and detail.

- A friendly work environment.

- Group activities outside the job.

- A manager who practices participative management.

- Freedom from routine work.

- A wide scope of activities.

- A support system to do the detail work.

- Changing environments in which to work/play.

- Outside activities so there is never a dull moment.

- Freedom to talk and participate on the team.

- Participation in meetings on future planning.

KEYS TO MANAGING

In this section are some needs which must be met in order for John to perform at an optimum level. Some needs can be met by himself, while management must provide for others. It is difficult for a person to enter a motivational environment when that person's basic management needs have not been fulfilled. Review the list with John and identify three or four statements that are most important to him. This allows John to participate in forming his own personal management plan.

John needs:

- To display empathy for people who approach life differently than he does.

- Objectivity when dealing with people because of his high trust level.

- People to work and associate with.

- A program for pacing work and relaxing.

- A rational approach to decision making—analyze the facts.

- More logical presentations—less emotional.

- More control of body language.

- Participatory management.

- To be confronted when in disagreement, or when he breaks the rules.

- To understand his role on the team—either a team player or the leader.

- To adjust his intensity to match the situation.

AREAS FOR IMPROVEMENT

In this area is a listing of possible limitations without regard to a specific job. Review with John and cross out those limitations that do not apply. Highlight one to three limitations that are hindering his performance and develop an action plan to eliminate or reduce this hindrance.

John has a tendency to:

- Have trouble delegating—can't wait, so does it himself.

- Resist participation as part of the team, unless seen as a leader.

- Be so concerned with big picture; he forgets to see the little pieces.

- Be disruptive because of his innate restlessness and disdain for sameness.

- Keep too many balls in the air, and if his support is weak he will have a tendency to drop some of those balls.

- Dislike routine work or routine people—unless he sees the need to further his goals.

- Fail to complete what he starts because of adding more and more projects.

- Be explosive by nature and lack the patience to negotiate.

- Be a one-way communicator—doesn't listen to the total story before introducing his opinion.

ACTION PLAN

Name: John Doe

The following are examples of areas in which John may want to improve. Circle one to three areas and develop action plan(s) to bring about the desired results. Look over the report for possible areas that need improvement.

Communicating (Listening)	Time Management
Delegating	Career Goals
Decision Making	Personal Goals
Disciplining	Motivating Others
Evaluating Performance	Developing People
Education	Family

Area:

1.

2.

3.

Area:

1.

2.

3.

Area:

1.

2.

3.

Date to Begin: _____ **Date to Review:** _____

BEHAVIORAL FACTOR INDICATOR™

Management Version

John Doe
12-4-2003

INTRODUCTION

Classifying management behavior is not an easy undertaking, largely because there are so many variables on which classifications could be based. The classifications in this report are purely behavioral. Behavioral measurement can be classified as how a person will do a job. No consideration has been given to age, experience, training, or values.

Your report will graphically display your behavioral skills in twelve specific factors. Each factor was carefully selected allowing anyone to be successful if they meet the behavioral demands of the job.

The Natural graph represents your natural behavior—the behavior you bring to the job. The Adapted graph measures your response to the environment—the behavior you think is necessary to succeed at a job. If your Adapted graph is significantly different from your Natural, you are under pressure to change or "mask" your behavior.

Read and compare your graphs. Look at each factor and the importance of that factor to the successful performance of your job. Your Adapted graph will identify the factors you see as important and shows you where you are focusing your energy.

Knowledge of your behavior will allow you to develop strategies to win in any environment you choose.

SPECIFIC FACTOR ANALYSIS

John Doe

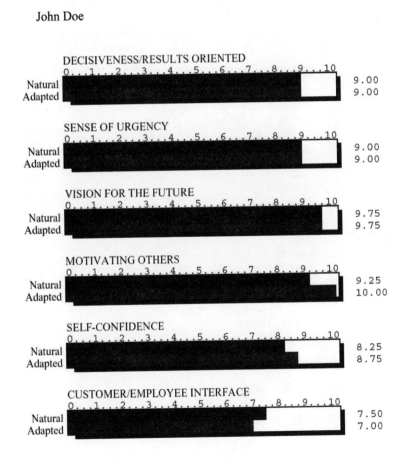

DECISIVENESS/RESULTS ORIENTED
0...1...2...3...4...5...6...7...8...9...10
Natural — 9.00
Adapted — 9.00

SENSE OF URGENCY
0...1...2...3...4...5...6...7...8...9...10
Natural — 9.00
Adapted — 9.00

VISION FOR THE FUTURE
0...1...2...3...4...5...6...7...8...9...10
Natural — 9.75
Adapted — 9.75

MOTIVATING OTHERS
0...1...2...3...4...5...6...7...8...9...10
Natural — 9.25
Adapted — 10.00

SELF-CONFIDENCE
0...1...2...3...4...5...6...7...8...9...10
Natural — 8.25
Adapted — 8.75

CUSTOMER/EMPLOYEE INTERFACE
0...1...2...3...4...5...6...7...8...9...10
Natural — 7.50
Adapted — 7.00

SPECIFIC FACTOR ANALYSIS

John Doe

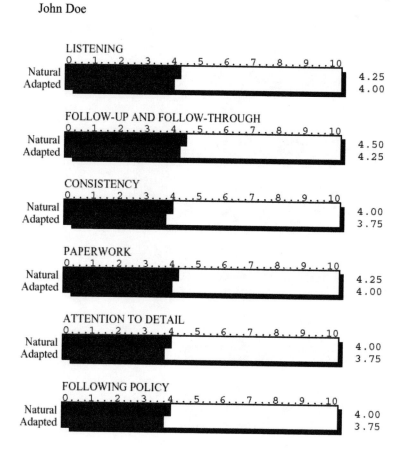

LISTENING

0...1...2...3...4...5...6...7...8...9...10

Natural — 4.25
Adapted — 4.00

FOLLOW-UP AND FOLLOW-THROUGH

0...1...2...3...4...5...6...7...8...9...10

Natural — 4.50
Adapted — 4.25

CONSISTENCY

0...1...2...3...4...5...6...7...8...9...10

Natural — 4.00
Adapted — 3.75

PAPERWORK

0...1...2...3...4...5...6...7...8...9...10

Natural — 4.25
Adapted — 4.00

ATTENTION TO DETAIL

0...1...2...3...4...5...6...7...8...9...10

Natural — 4.00
Adapted — 3.75

FOLLOWING POLICY

0...1...2...3...4...5...6...7...8...9...10

Natural — 4.00
Adapted — 3.75

STYLE ANALYSIS™ GRAPHS

John Doe
12-4-2003

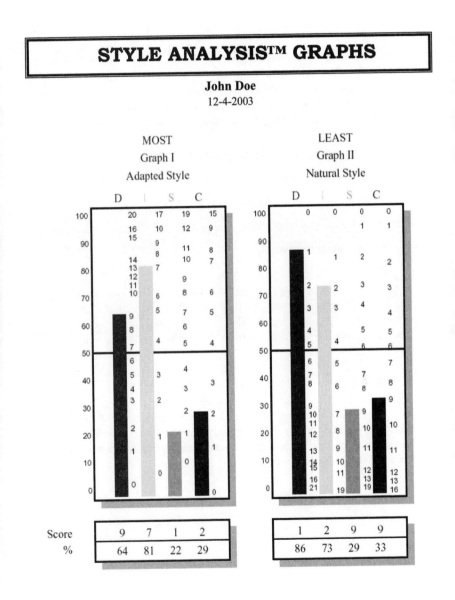

THE SUCCESS INSIGHTS® WHEEL

The Success Insights® Wheel is a powerful tool popularized in Europe. In addition to the text you have received about your behavioral style, the Wheel adds a visual representation that allows you to:

- View your natural behavioral style (circle).

- View your adapted behavioral style (star).

- Note the degree you are adapting your behavior.

- If you filled out the Work Environment Analysis, view the relationship of your behavior to your job.

Notice on the next page that your Natural style (circle) and your Adapted style (star) are plotted on the Wheel. If they are plotted in different boxes, then you are adapting your behavior. The further the two plotting points are from each other, the more you are adapting your behavior.

If you are part of a group or team who also took the behavioral assessment, it would be advantageous to get together, using each person's Wheel, and make a master Wheel that contains each person's Natural and Adapted style. This allows you to quickly see where conflict can occur. You will also be able to identify where communication, understanding, and appreciation can be increased.

THE SUCCESS INSIGHTS® WHEEL

John Doe
12-4-2003

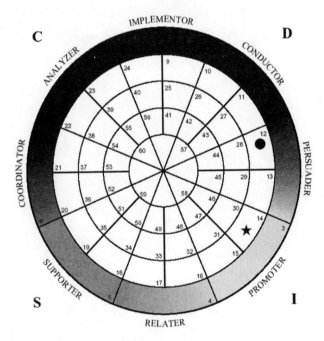

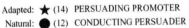
Adapted: ★ (14) PERSUADING PROMOTER
Natural: ● (12) CONDUCTING PERSUADER

MANAGING FOR SUCCESS®

Personal Interests, Attitudes, and Values™

"He who knows others is
learned.
He who knows himself is
wise."
–Lao Tse

John Doe
12-4-2003

UNDERSTANDING YOUR REPORT

Knowledge of an individual's attitudes help to tell us WHY they do things. A review of an individual's experiences, references, education, and training help to tell us WHAT they can do. Behavioral assessments help to tell us HOW a person behaves and performs in the work environment. The PIAV report measures the relative prominence of six basic interests or attitudes (a way of valuing life): Theoretical, Utilitarian, Aesthetic, Social, Individualistic, and Traditional.

Attitudes help to initiate one's behavior and are sometimes called the hidden motivators because they are not always readily observed. It is the purpose of this report to help illuminate and amplify some of those motivating factors and to build on the strengths that each person brings to the work environment.

Based on your choices, this report ranks your relative passion for each of the six attitudes. Your top two and sometimes three attitudes cause you to move into action. You will feel positive when talking, listening, or doing activities that satisfy your top attitudes.

The feedback you will receive in this section will reflect one of three intensity levels for each of the six attitudes.

• STRONG—positive feelings that you need to satisfy either on or off the job.

• SITUATIONAL—where your feelings will range from positive to indifferent based on other priorities in your life at the time. These attitudes tend to become more important as your top attitudes are satisfied.

• INDIFFERENT—your feelings will be indifferent when related to your 5th or 6th attitude.

YOUR ATTITUDES RANKING		
1st	UTILITARIAN	Strong
2nd	THEORETICAL	Strong
3rd	INDIVIDUALISTIC	Situational
4th	TRADITIONAL	Situational
5th	AESTHETIC	Indifferent
6th	SOCIAL	Indifferent

UTILITARIAN

The Utilitarian score shows a characteristic interest in money and what is useful. This means that an individual wants to have the security that money brings not only for themselves, but for their present and future family. This value includes the practical affairs of the business world—the production, marketing, and consumption of goods, the use of credit, and the accumulation of tangible wealth. This type of individual is thoroughly practical and conforms well to the stereotype of the average American businessperson. A person with a high score is likely to have a high need to surpass others in wealth.

- John will protect his assets to ensure the future of his economic security.

- Having more wealth than others is a high priority for John.

- He can be very practical.

- All attempts are made to protect future security to ensure that his legacy is protected.

- Wealth provides the security John wants for himself and/or his family.

- John faces the future confidently.

- John will attempt to structure his economic dealings.

- John has a long list of wants and will work hard to achieve them.

- With economic security comes the freedom to advance his ideas or beliefs.

- John will be motivated by his accomplishments.

- He uses money as a scorecard.

THEORETICAL

The primary drive with this value is the discovery of TRUTH. In pursuit of this value, an individual takes a "cognitive" attitude. Such an individual is nonjudgmental regarding the beauty or utility of objects and seeks only to observe and to reason. Since the interests of the theoretical person are empirical, critical, and rational, the person appears to be an intellectual. The chief aim in life is to order and systematize knowledge: knowledge for the sake of knowledge.

- A comfortable job for John is one that challenges his knowledge.

- John has the potential to become an expert in his chosen field.

- John is comfortable around people who share his interest for knowledge and especially those people with similar convictions.

- He will usually have the data to support his convictions.

- John is very good at integrating past knowledge to solve present problems.

- He may have difficulty putting down a good book.

INDIVIDUALISTIC

The primary interest for this value is POWER, not necessarily politics. Research studies indicate that leaders in most fields have a high power value. Since competition and struggle play a large part in all areas of life, many philosophers have seen power as the most universal and most fundamental of motives. There are, however, certain personalities in whom the desire for direct expression of this motive is uppermost; who wish, above all, for personal power, influence, and renown.

- He will evaluate each situation individually and determine how much or how little control he will want to exercise.

- John can be assertive in meeting his needs.

- At times John can be very competitive.

- The amount of control he attempts will increase if he has strong feelings about the issues involved with the situation. If, however, he has little interest in the issues involved, he will not see the need for exercising control.

TRADITIONAL

The highest interest for this value may be called "unity," "order," or "tradition." Individuals with high scores in this value seek a system for living. This system can be found in such things as religion, conservatism or any authority that has defined rules, regulations, and principles for living.

- John needs to be able to pick and choose the traditions and set of beliefs to which he will adhere.

- John at times will evaluate others based on his rules for living.

- John lets his conscience be his guide.

- He will have strong beliefs within a system that he feels most comfortable with, and he will not be as strong in his beliefs or approach if he lacks that interest level.

AESTHETIC

*A higher Aesthetic score indicates a relative interest in "form and harmony."
Each experience is judged from the standpoint of grace, symmetry, or fitness. Life
may be regarded as a procession of events, and each is enjoyed for its own sake. A
high score here does not necessarily mean that the incumbent has talents in
creative artistry. It indicates a primary interest in the artistic episodes of life.*

- John is not necessarily worried about form and beauty in his environment.

- John's passion in life will be found in one or two of the other attitudes
  and values discussed in this report.

- Intellectually, John can see the need for beauty, but has difficulty buying
  the finer things in life.

- The utility of "something" is more important than its beauty, form, and
  harmony.

- Unpleasant surroundings will not stifle his creativity.

- He wants to take a practical approach to events.

- He is a very practical person who is not sensitive to being in harmony
  with his surroundings.

SOCIAL

Those who score very high in this value have an inherent love of people. The social person prizes other people and is, therefore, kind, sympathetic, and unselfish. They are likely to find the Theoretical, Utilitarian, and Aesthetic attitudes cold and inhuman. Compared to the Individualistic value, the Social person regards helping others as the only suitable form for human relationships. Research into this value indicates that in its purest form, the Social interest is selfless.

- John is willing to help others if they are working as hard as possible to achieve their goals.

- John's passion in life will be found in one or two of the other dimensions discussed in this report.

- He will be firm in his decisions and not be swayed by unfortunate circumstances.

- Believing that hard work and persistence is within everyone's reach, he feels things must be earned, not given.

- He will not normally allow himself to be directed by others unless it will enhance his own self-interest.

- John will be torn if helping others proves to be detrimental to him.

ATTITUDES – NORMS & COMPARISONS

For years you have heard statements like, "Different strokes for different folks," "to each his own," and "people do things for their own reasons, not yours." When you are surrounded by people who share similar attitudes, you will fit in with the group and be energized. However, when surrounded by people whose attitudes are significantly different from yours, you may be perceived as out of the mainstream. These differences can induce stress or conflict. When confronted with this type of situation you can:

- Change the situation.
- Change your perception of the situation.
- Leave the situation.
- Cope with the situation.

This section reveals areas where your attitudes may be outside the mainstream and could lead to conflict. The further away you are from the mainstream on the high side, the more people will notice your passion about that attitude. The further away from the mainstream on the low side, the more people will view you as indifferent and possibly negative about that attitude. The shaded area for each attitude represents 68 percent of the population or scores that fall within one standard deviation above or below the national mean.

NORMS & COMPARISONS TABLE John Doe		
THEORETICAL	*	Mainstream
UTILITARIAN	*	Passionate
AESTHETIC	*	Mainstream
SOCIAL	*	Indifferent
INDIVIDUALISTIC	*	Passionate
TRADITIONAL	*	Indifferent

▮ - 68 percent of the population

| - national mean

* - your score

Mainstream—one standard deviation of the national mean
Passionate—two standard deviations above the national mean
Indifferent—two standard deviations below the national mean
Extreme—three standard deviations from the national mean

ATTITUDES – NORMS & COMPARISONS

Areas in which you have strong feelings or passions compared to others:

- You strive for efficiency and practicality in all areas of your life, seeking to gain a return on your investment of time, talent, and resources. Others may feel you always have a string attached and are always trying to gain a personal advantage. They may feel you should give just for the sake of giving.

- You have a strong desire to lead, direct, and control your own destiny and the destiny of others. You have a desire to lead and are striving for opportunities to advance your position and influence. Others may believe you are jockeying for position and continually stepping "over the line." They may believe that you form relationships only to "move ahead" and gain an advantage.

Areas where others' strong feelings may frustrate you as you do not share their same passion:

- Your self-reliance will cause you to feel uncomfortable around people who are always trying to help you or be too nice to you.

- Others who try to impose their way of living on you will frustrate you. Your ability to try new things frustrates them and they feel compelled to change you to their system.

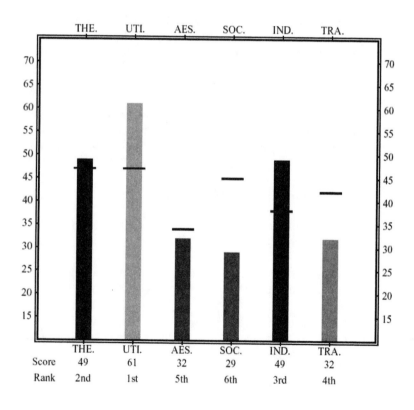

ATTITUDES GRAPH

John Doe
5-7-2001

ATTITUDES WHEEL

John Doe
5-7-2001

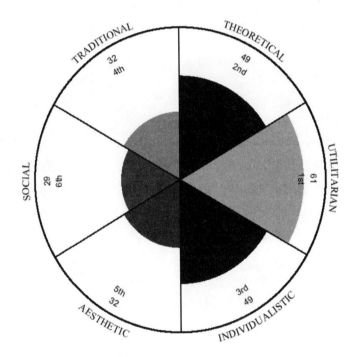

Development Plan Summary

Organization:	Client Name:	Date:

List the *behavioral strengths* identified in the employee's profile:
1.
2.
3.

List the *behavioral blind spots* identified in the employee's profile:
1.
2.
3.

What are the areas that the employee would like to improve in:
Communicating
Listening
Delegating
Decision Making
Evaluating Performance
Disciplining
Time Management
Career Goals
Personal Goals
Motivating Others
Developing People

What action steps will the employee take to improve in these areas? (What do they need to start, stop, or continue doing or modify to improve in these areas?):

- _____
- _____
- _____
- _____
- _____
- _____

What are the top attributes that the employee has committed to working on?

- _____
- _____
- _____
- _____

What are the attributes/scores that the employee had the most difficulty with?

- _____
- _____
- _____
- _____

Action steps:

- _____
- _____
- _____
- _____
- _____
- _____

How will you measure your progress?

- _____
- _____
- _____
- _____
- _____

CHAPTER 8

Retaining High-Maintenance Employees

*"That which we persist in doing becomes easier for us to do;
not that the nature of the thing itself is changed,
but that our power to do it is increased."*

—Albert Einstein

In this chapter, learn to retain your high-maintenance employees by:
- Setting them up for success
- Motivating, rewarding, and recognizing them in ways that are most effective with this personality type
- Knowing what kind of management might cause them to leave

Perhaps you've noticed lately that an employee who you consider to be a top performer on your team is restless. As noted previously, getting bored easily is very characteristic of a HMHP, a problem that is especially apt to occur at the completion of a project. The last time this happened, you said to yourself, "I'm never going to let this occur again because this person is too valuable to lose. I'm going to make sure I do what it takes so that my HMHP is happy."

Does this sound familiar? If so, you need to read further about how to retain your high-maintenance employees or learn how to safeguard so they don't get bored and restless again. If this hasn't happened yet to you, and you're working with high-maintenance employees, it will. Just give it time.

Your worries about losing your high-maintenance employees are common in today's business environment. The retention game has changed in the twenty-first century; what made high-maintenance employees stay in a job ten to twenty years ago won't necessarily prompt them to stay at your company today. Research conducted by Kaye and Jordan-Evans shows that the following opportunities actually made high performers stay. Their findings were ranked in the order of preference.

- Exciting work and challenges
- Career growth, learning, and development
- Great people
- Fair pay
- Good boss
- Recognition and valued respect
- Benefits
- Meaningful work and opportunity to make a difference
- Pride in organization, mission, and its products/services
- Great work environment/culture

Excelling in all of these areas in your company is a challenge, yet doing so is essential, as noted by many top executive leaders. At the Leadership Speaks Conference in 2004, an executive leadership survey was reported on that asked close to 1000 CEOs, senior executives, and business owners to submit their top three business challenges for tomorrow, and they replied:

- Retaining the right people
- Hiring the right people
- Generating profitable growth

Jack Welch, former president and CEO of General Electric, said that one of the many reasons he was successful at GE was because the company spends time on developing its talent, the high performers.

In creating a work environment that adapts to the needs of

FCO|Footnote Reference|FCC| *Kaye, Beverly and Sharon Jordan-Evans, Love 'Em or Lose 'Em: Getting Good People to Stay* high-maintenance employees, there are two aspects critical to the likelihood that they will remain satisfied and stay with your company: motivating and rewarding them.

One senior management team of twenty people that I worked with included approximately six high-maintenance employees. As I met with each HMHP manager individually, a common theme emerged. Each manager talked about how the president and the people above them tended to micromanage. They would be asked for solutions to specific problems; which vendors to use, which people to hire, and so on. Then, very often, their suggestions were disregarded. Not only were their ideas ignored, but upper management sometimes came back later to implement the same solution that one of these high-maintenance employees initially had presented. The high-maintenance employees often felt that the rug had been pulled out from underneath them.

These high-maintenance employees liked activity. They like to be moving and they often felt like things were stalled because upper management was making the decisions, or they hadn't made the decisions yet, or they were still just preparing to make the decisions.

This team was very frustrated by the fact that they didn't have the freedom, control, and autonomy to lead their teams. What upper management did not get was that these high-maintenance employees were most productive and self-motivated when they were working on innovative solutions to problems and were given the autonomy to do it.

Motivating or Self-Motivating

I often say that you cannot motivate someone. When I speak in front of a group and say that, the managers often challenge me. "What do you mean?" they ask. "That's my job. What do you mean I can't motivate someone?" My reply is that you cannot motivate someone else because ultimately all people are self-motivated.

And self-motivation is often more apparent in high-maintenance employees than in the other behavioral styles.

Managers then ask, "If you can't motivate someone, what can you do?" What you can do is hold people accountable. People are motivated to do what they want to do, not what you want them to do. So a lot of time gets wasted trying to manage high-maintenance employees by attempting to motivate them, something that is quite impossible to do.

One of the chief ingredients for retaining high-maintenance employees, then, is to create an environment where they feel self-motivated. You also need to make sure that the manager's goals and those of the HMHP are the same and that the HMHP owns those goals. If this isn't the case, high-maintenance employees will end up doing what they want to do.

Here are the elements of an environment that makes the most of the self-motivation of high-maintenance employees:

Controlling their own destiny

First, you need to allow high-maintenance employees to control their own destiny. They want to feel autonomous; they want to feel independent. They want to feel they have some control over the solution that is going to lead to the desired results. They are quick decision makers and prefer to work for those who can make quick decisions as well, so they don't feel held back.

As a HMHP, I was happiest at my job and performing at my best when I was told what the outcome needed to be and given the autonomy to set up my own structure for operating. And I was able to plan my work and work my plan. When I was working someone else's plan, I became extremely frustrated. It was easier to share, report on, and explain a plan that I had brought forth on my own.

Providing your high-maintenance employees with opportunities to work independently or allowing them to direct the efforts of others creates an environment where they feel more control over their destiny.

Tip: Give high-maintenance employees control over their destiny, and they will become comfortable and share their plans.

Earlier in this chapter I spoke of high-maintenance employees who were telling me how they would submit a plan to do something and then upper management would change it. They felt they had absolutely no control over their destiny because they were forced to use vendors that they wouldn't have chosen. When they were in a situation where they were given the autonomy to choose the vendors they wanted to use and operate in a way that they wanted, they became highly productive. Then they would also take more responsibility for the performance of those vendors. They owned the objective and the results.

Tip: Give your high-maintenance employees the autonomy to choose their plan and resources, and they will take greater responsibility for the results.

I do a lot of work with self-directed work teams consisting of high-maintenance employees. They tend to be teams of people who are capable of working effectively without being led by others. So when upper management comes in and tells them the policy they have to follow, they get very frustrated, because they want to be empowered to set up the structure that they feel works for them. And oftentimes the structure they set up involves higher standards than the one management would have set up anyway.

Tip: Give your high-maintenance employees the opportunity to set their own goals; they will often set higher standards than otherwise would be expected.

Authority to achieve results

You will help your high-maintenance employees build an environment for self-motivation if you also give them the power and the authority. High-maintenance employees need basic principles to follow. They are not process oriented by nature. The non-high-maintenance employees tend to possess more of the process-oriented characteristics. High-maintenance employees will need support but not regulations to achieve their goals.

> Tip: Give your high-maintenance employees the autonomy to set up their own structure for pursuing their goals; they often find a more efficient way to operate and to achieve those goals.

Feed their need to compete

High-maintenance employees love to win and hate to lose. When I talk about self-realization or self-actualization as it relates to high-maintenance employees, I am talking about their competitive nature. They tend to be more competitive with themselves than they are with anyone else. The recognition, the rewards, the autonomy to achieve results taps into the self-realization they need in order to feel they are making a difference and to feel they are valued. Making high-maintenance employees feel that they are valued and making a difference, and telling them often, is important for promoting their self-motivation. It goes back to how they are harder on themselves than anybody else. To the world it may appear as though they are highly competitive with this person or this group or this organization, and some of that might be true, but it all starts with themselves.

> **Tip:** Feed the competitive nature of the high-maintenance employee to get better results from them.

Accountability for results

Hold your high-maintenance employees accountable for the outcome, not the process. As I've said, they tend not to be concerned with the details. This is not their strength.

Here's an example with sales people. I was coaching a manager, a vice president of sales, who tended to be very structured. He was very analytical by nature. Even though he was great at sales, he felt there was a right way and a wrong way of doing things. He tended to encourage people to follow his way, the so-called "right way," instead of giving people the freedom to use their own process. He kept assigning the process to his high-maintenance employees instead of letting them come up with their own map. He lost people over it. His team was very frustrated. As a matter of fact, people felt he wasn't approachable because he wasn't flexible enough to hear that someone might have another way of approaching a problem to get to the same results.

An improvement summary is an effective tool for helping high-maintenance employees focus on improving their performance without being too restrictive about the processes they use. This summary lists the competencies an individual needs to perform his or her job adequately. A manager reviews the competencies with an individual and rates how well the individual is performing on each. The summary identifies which competencies the individual needs to improve. It is a way to review goals and continually set new challenges that will pave the way for success. A sample improvement summary is included at the end of this chapter.

> Tip: Continually encourage your high-maintenance employees to set new goals. This encourages growth and gives them a path to excel.

Rewarding

Prestige, position, and titles

All employees, not just high-maintenance employees, want to feel valued. Part of what helps high-maintenance employees feel valued is their status. Whenever you walk into the office of a HMHP, you will see certifications, certificates, diplomas, and other symbols that represent prestige. They like to display their position and their title. It helps them to feel valued, to feel important. Non-high-maintenance employees care less about this. It is not that important to them. In previous chapters, I discuss how high-maintenance employees will thrive in leading a project, program, or team, if they are managed correctly. This ties into the overall results; that's prestige for them. Adding words like "Senior" to their titles if they've been there for a long time will go a long way in retaining your high-maintenance employees.

> Tip: Title is important to HMHPs and challenges them to achieve.

Group activities outside the job

High-maintenance employees like a lot of activity. They like a lot of things going on at once. They tend to have short attention spans. Often people will say, "Are you listening to me?" And their minds are racing on to the next thing. So lots of activity is engaging for them. And holding their attention for long periods of time isn't that easy.

High-maintenance employees need to be connected to the outside world. They tend to give everything to their jobs. One HMHP told us about her experience. She had a horrendous work schedule, working an average seventy-five-hour week. On top of that, she always took a course at the local university. Her friends thought she was crazy. They would ask, "How can you do that?" And she would say, "You don't understand. I need to. I need to know that I'm doing something for myself to move myself forward in another direction."

Most high-maintenance employees need to have something else going on. Reward them with opportunities for outside achievements that are related to their job or in some way that moves them forward on their career path or some growth path. They are so committed and dedicated to what they are doing that there has to be some other outlet that they have, but it still needs to be tied into achieving something.

Tip: Provide ways to build on their skills through outside activities or training, to create a supportive environment for their active behavior.

Popularity and recognition

By nature most high-maintenance employees want to be liked. This could mean liked in terms of respect and it could mean liked socially by other people. There is a difference. Some high-maintenance employees don't care so much about being liked; they care about respect.

High-maintenance employees want to shine in public. They want their names to appear somewhere that's public. They want visibility, they want recognition, they like it publicly. Non-high-maintenance employees, on the other hand, often are not as comfortable receiving public recognition. They prefer recognition one-on-one.

Tip: Make their accomplishments public.

Monetary rewards

High-maintenance employees think of things in terms of having value. They see themselves as having value and they want to be rewarded based on that value. So they use it as a yardstick measure. They are competitive. These rewards are part of their self-motivation.

Consequently it is extremely important to have an evaluation system in place. How often are you evaluating and measuring performance? Some of the most common measurement and evaluation tools include:

- Biannual or Annual Performance Standards/Reviews/ Appraisals: These usually include quantitative and qualitative sections where both the employee and manager have opportunities to make remarks. They state expectations and goals. The employee's performance is measured against these goals at the end of the time period. Traditionally, these appraisals are directly tied to annual bonuses or pay increases.
- Budget/Quota Measurements: These include measuring a person's performance against budget expectations and quotas. The person is evaluated based on how well he/she performed, and rewards are directly tied to performance.

Tip: Make sure that their monetary rewards are on par with where they believe they should be.

What Not to Do with High-Maintenance Employees

Now let's take a look at what will most likely lessen the job satisfaction of your high-maintenance employees. Behaviors that will create tension or dissatisfaction in managing your high-maintenance employees include:

- Talking about things that are not relevant to the issue

- Leaving loopholes or cloudy issues
- Appearing disorganized
- Being curt, cold, or tight-lipped
- Controlling the conversation
- Driving on facts and figures, alternatives, and abstractions

Behaviors like these make high-maintenance employees feel that they are being micromanaged or that their contributions are not being recognized. Feeling out of control of their destiny, they are apt to jump ship, leaving a significant hole in your organization.

Create an Environment for Your High-Maintenance Employees to Thrive In

The following is a list to help you create an environment so that they are contributing all of their positive characteristics in a positive and profitable way.

This may be a list that you want to come back to to make sure that you are creating an environment to get the most out of your high-maintenance employees.

Here is a quick summary of the ways in which you can create an environment where your high-maintenance employees will thrive:

- Allow them to control their own destiny and the destiny of others.
- Give them power and authority to achieve results.
- Provide prestige, position, and titles.
- Provide them with a vehicle to obtain money and material things that indicate success.
- Allow the opportunity for rapid advancement.
- Allow freedom from controls, supervision, and details.
- Provide challenges with each task.
- Provide new and varied experiences.
- Assist in setting realistic goals.
- Work with them on their on time-management.
- Develop a friendship and make time for interaction daily.
- Create an open door policy to discuss any issues.

• Set clear objectives of the task to be accomplished.

• Look for opportunities for them to utilize their verbal skills.

In the next chapter, we'll delve deeper into the leadership style that works best with high-maintenance employees. It's simple and it's logical. People will be more productive and get better results when they are managed the way they prefer to be managed. The more we communicate to others in a way they prefer to receive it, the more likely it is they'll receive it.

Continuous Improvement Summary Worksheet

Employee Name:			
Skills	Exceeds Standards	At Standards	Below Standard
Employee Competencies			
Self-Management			
Service			
Persuasion			
Written Communication			
Diplomacy			
Goal Orientation			
Teamwork			
Commitment			
Handling Stress			
Problem Solving			
Interpersonal Skills			
Flexibility			
Presenting			
Planning/Organizing			
Empathy			
Negotiating Skills			
High Tolerance for Frustration			
Self-Awareness			
Self-Confidence			
Assertiveness			
Integrity			
Project and Goal Focus			
Other:			
Other:			

Design an improvement summary for your high-maintenance employees by using the competencies outlined above. Please begin this process by defining each competency as it relates to your organization.

CHAPTER 9

Working for a High-Maintenance, High Performer Boss

"The person who knows how will always have a job.
The person who knows why will always be his boss."

—Diane Ravitch

In this chapter, you'll learn:
- What to expect if you have a HMHP boss, including those behaviors that you may find frustrating if your behavioral style is different
- Tips for working successfully with a HMHP boss
- What behaviors will frustrate a HMHP boss

One day you'll walk into your HMHP boss's office and she will be very friendly. She'll say, "Sit down... How was your weekend? How is your family? How are you doing?" The next day you'll walk into her office and her responses will be short and intense. And you'll say to yourself, "Where is the person that I saw yesterday?"

Often the HMHP boss can appear a bit schizophrenic. When in task mode, a HMHP tends to be very, very focused. Recall from prior chapters that high-maintenance employees are intense by nature and the more stress or pressure they're under or the more they have on their plate, the less likely they are to chitchat and talk.

Here are tips that will help you solve the riddle of your HMHP boss.

Tip #1: Get Down to Business

You have to look for the signs. When high-maintenance bosses want to chitchat, they'll let you know. So you'll do better if you watch for clues from your HMHP boss before assuming he or she is in the mood to chat.

In fact, the HMHP boss's sense of urgency and drive can be very difficult to work with, especially if you're the type of person who tends to get caught up in the analytical side of things or if you don't like change. If you tend to get stuck in the process or have trouble with change, that style tends to conflict more strongly with HMHP bosses, who thrive on change and can be very impatient by nature.

For this reason, you think the analytical work you're doing is important. It's critical that you communicate to your HMHP boss what the benefit and result will be in your approach.

Be sure to deliver your project on the agreed time frame because your HMHP boss does not want to be slowed down by missed deadlines. Even though HMHP bosses love and thrive on creativity and appreciate the people who bring innovation into the work environment, it's important to tie your creative development and innovation to a result and a specific time frame.

HMHP bosses want to get to the finish line. Most of the time HMHP bosses are moving very quickly. So they won't want to listen to a lot of counterarguments. However, slower moving, process-oriented people are a good fit for HMHP bosses, because they help the HMHP boss think through the process, options, and consequences of plans and decisions, which is what they tend not to be very good at. Be sure to keep suggestions very brief, ordered from most to least important, and stated as benefits or results.

Tip #2: Don't Take It Personally!

HMHP bosses tend to think out loud. They turn ideas over in rapid fire, juggle multiple scenarios, and think about the present while exploring the future. You have to remember not to take what they say and how they say it personally because so often the intensity you hear isn't directed at you. Their intensity and passion for business may seem cold and distant to others. It's their internal motivation for getting things right and their need to be moving in the right direction at all times that often creates this intensity.

Often HMHP bosses go with their instincts. If their instincts tell them something isn't right, they will appear even more intense and uncomfortable. To others, this comes across as moodiness.

If you get this type of reaction when presenting a plan or status report to your HMHP boss, it can be a clue that it's not going well. In such a case, you may want to stop and ask for input from your boss so you can discern the true cause of this intensity. If the boss is uncomfortable with the direction you're headed in, you want to know that as soon as possible.

HMHP bosses are emotional, talk out loud, and tell you directly what they think. Adjusting to this can be hard for people who are not used to direct communicators. Always listen, evaluate, and question when the comment or direction is not clear or appears inaccurate. Being direct communicators, HMHP bosses appreciate direct feedback and questions.

Tip #3: Give Your HMHP Boss Only Essential Details

While many high-maintenance bosses love to learn and are driven to learn, most of the time they want to take a practical approach by using the information that they learned. They want to be able to do something with it. So, providing excessive details does not work with the HMHP boss. These bosses want to know exactly what they need to know, when they need it, and then they want to move on.

Therefore, don't bog them down with a lot of detail when presenting ideas or reports to them. Always start with the benefits: how will it benefit the company, how will it benefit the goal, how will it benefit the customers. Then talk about the relevant specifics and attach all of your supporting detail for them to read later if they want to.

I was working with a division vice president who was having trouble communicating with her HMHP boss. When presenting to her HMHP boss, she would start off with all of the analytical detail, then every detail in the process, and at the end of the presentation she would present the benefits and why the organization should contribute the resources to do the program. To her, she was building a logical case for her proposal. But it was obvious her boss wasn't listening.

After working with her, I flipped her presentation so that it started with the benefits and attached all of the detail. After the presentation, her HMHP boss said it was the best presentation that she had ever done. This is a great way to communicate with a HMHP boss.

Tip #4: Figure out What Your High-maintenance Boss Wants

Most high-maintenance bosses want respect from those they work with. They want to be seen as the expert on their subject matter. Their image is important to them. And while they might not be very good at the details, they are good at how things look and there is a way they want things to look. It's your job to gather the information and get some clarity around what it is they're looking for. They're not always great at communicating what they want or specifically how they want it, so you have to figure it out by asking the right questions. Ask direct questions and ask them often. Update your high-maintenance boss to make sure that you are on track at the beginning, middle, and end of a project.

Tip #5: Always Approach Your HMHP Boss with Solutions

Jim Collins, author of *Good to Great*, says, "Leaders have humility, they have will, they can look in the window and look at themselves." HMHP bosses tend to put the blame on themselves rather than on other people. Nine times out of ten, when a mistake is made and it's something that they can't solve, they'll take the blame themselves. They are very hard on themselves.

One of the misperceptions of working for HMHP bosses is that they get very frustrated and are intolerant when mistakes are made. They have very high standards, and most of the time they have trouble living up to their own standards. So how is anybody else going to? If you make a mistake, be prepared to talk about it, and have solutions for fixing it ready to suggest.

Think through the process and come up with ideas on how to solve the problem yourself. Don't be afraid to approach your HMHP boss even if you don't think you have great ideas. Communicating without an option will be viewed by your boss as a waste of time. Options work better for a HMHP boss than no options at all.

HMHP bosses by nature are very creative problem solvers. If at first they can't figure something out, they don't give up until they do. After you reach a consensus on the right solution, then you can decide what process you want to take to get to the desired end result. Your HMHP boss will see this as extremely valuable.

Tip #6: Look for the Best Product, Fastest Way to Implement, or Latest Technology for Your Recommended Solution

Most of the presidents and CEOs I work with always ask me, "What is the best organization system that you've ever used? Got any ideas of great programs out there?" They are always looking for the tool that's going to make them more efficient.

Remember, high-maintenance bosses prefer options. They want to know that they have the best option available to help them operate as efficiently as possible. Use bullet points and brief statements when recommending your solutions and always begin with the benefits.

High-maintenance bosses want the best and won't settle for anything that's just mediocre. If they view something as the best, they'll figure out how to get it. They definitely want to operate efficiently. They know the necessity of details and they want to be sure they are considering the right details even though that's not their greatest strength. Helping them identify what is best and why will be viewed as very useful.

Tip #7: Establish a Timeline and Priority for Projects and Requests

How do you stay two steps ahead of a HMHP boss? Well, you don't. You always want to be looking ahead and communicating what's coming up. Make it your job to communicate, not theirs.

One of the most difficult things about working for HMHP bosses is their tendency to like the latest and greatest, newest idea. When they get the new idea, they want to make it happen. Just last week you may have been moving in one direction or working on one initiative, only to find this week you are presented with another.

Unfortunately, when HMHP bosses ask for something, they mean now. So it's important that you always get a deadline. To make sure you set a realistic deadline, set it yourself. You can say, "Okay, this is what you need; this is when I'm going to get it to you." Do not leave a project open ended.

Do what you say you're going to do. If you can't, make sure you communicate what the obstacles are to your HMHP boss. HMHP bosses are problem solvers by nature. They will help you when presented with options. Ask for help.

Working for a HMHP boss, you really need to clarify the timeline and the expectations. Don't assume. Communicate, communicate, communicate. Most of the time, HMHP bosses don't mind your getting in their face. They become concerned when you don't ask questions. They would rather have you ask the questions and be thorough, because this is the way they tend to operate. And by being thorough, I don't mean in an absurd or annoying way. Just don't assume; when there is any possibility of ambiguity, always ask questions.

Change is also a difficult issue when it comes to timelines. Process-oriented people tend not to want to change things the way high-maintenance employees do. Reluctance to change will be viewed negatively unless it is accompanied by options and sound reasons. Often a better approach to questioning change or implementing something new is to create a timeline and then use it to establish priorities. It is a very effective way of highlighting just how much activity everyone is engaged in, especially when the HMHP boss creates a work overload.

I coached one HMHP boss who is the CEO and president of a $150 million company. Oftentimes he would direct the organization to do a new project. And while that project was in the works, he'd then attempt to get another project underway. After about a six-month period, they had about thirty projects in the works. The high-maintenance boss didn't realize how many projects were backed up. He was very frustrated because he didn't feel things were being moved along.

Because HMHP bosses can juggle a lot of things at the same time, they think everyone else can, too. It's important to show the HMHP boss what the process, staff requirements, and timelines are for each new project. Come to a consensus on the project deadline and its priority.

In this particular instance, we were able to coach this president and CEO, who had no idea how frustrated his people were feeling. He was so intense, there were times his people were afraid to approach him. How could they possibly say something couldn't be done?

To HMHP bosses, "can't" isn't a part of their vocabulary; "figure out another way" is. So this particular leader couldn't hear the word "can't," even if someone had the nerve to say it. Without any glimpse of reality or how things were stacking up, he would communicate with his people by saying, "Well let's just figure out how to get this done."

One of the most difficult things about working for HMHP bosses is that they tend to never "turn it off." Expect HMHP bosses to be working evenings and weekends. That doesn't mean they expect you to. They just want to know you're on top of your game; be sure you are ready with the highlights of the latest important information at a moment's notice.

Tip #8: Don't Surprise Your High-Maintenance Boss

While no boss appreciates being blind-sided or surprised by unexpected news, high-maintenance bosses are very sensitive to being kept informed about what it is they should know. It has to do with their need to be prepared and stay two steps ahead of everyone else about what is going on. If you feel as though your high-maintenance boss is micromanaging you, make sure you create opportunities for sharing the latest relevant information in a way that is direct and succinct. Over-communicate with your high-maintenance boss. Give him or her the information that they need to know to help them see the big picture. High-maintenance people are emotional and demanding. Keep them informed along the way.

Tip #9: Show Loyalty for Your HMHP Boss

For most HMHP bosses, loyalty is highly valued: loyalty to the project, to the job, to the company, and to the boss. They tend to commit themselves completely to whatever it is they do. They must trust the people around them. They both appreciate and want loyalty from those they manage. They in turn will be loyal to you.

How do you show your loyalty? You can show your loyalty by keeping your boss informed, by making sure that he or she gets the information to keep them on top of things. Bring your solutions to problems or new ideas to him or her first. Publicize your accomplishments, and do it in a way that makes your boss look good. Everyone likes to look good, don't they? Most important, do what you say you're going to do, and get it done when you say you'll get it done. Delivering on what you promise is important because it gets to the core of loyalty: trust. Loyalty is based on trust.

Tip #10: Make Sure Your HMHP Boss Knows Your Strengths

Make sure your HMHP boss is perfectly clear on those things that you not only love to do but also that you're really good at. Make it a point to be on the same page as your HMHP boss when it comes to your strengths and talents. Your HMHP boss will be instrumental in not only helping you grow in that particular area, but will also be sure to use the strengths that you possess. Focus your boss on the things you do really well. Be innovative and creative when you can so you can speak their language.

Jack Welch appears to be a typical HMHP boss. During his tenure as president and CEO at GE, he instituted a program whereby every ninety days each employee in the company submitted their best idea for that particular quarter. What happened was people at all levels in the organization gave their best ideas and an environment of innovation was instituted throughout the company as a result.

Tip #11: Communicate Your Successes and Your Wins

Whether you use the model Jack Welch used at GE or another, you should also communicate the highlights of your successes to your HMHP boss on a regular basis. Many times when I'm doing team building, I ask team members to talk about successes on a monthly basis. Each person submits one success or accomplishment, which then rolls up into a single communication from the team to the boss. Giving your HMHP boss a list of successes is the best way to get recognition for you, the team, and even your boss. It will also help you feel valued.

Remember that high-maintenance bosses by nature are not warm and fuzzy. They have to work hard at thinking about the human element. It is not natural for them.

I was talking to a HMHP boss and she mentioned that the names of all the employees are printed next to all of the doors throughout her office. She felt that was so helpful because she often doesn't remember names, but she knows she needs to be able to connect with her people.

She mentioned how she was in the cafeteria during lunch time standing in line with one of the employees and she happened to say to him, "Hey, I saw something you did; you did a really excellent job." She said this guy looked at her like she had just given him gold. She understood later how much it meant to that employee that she told him one-on-one what a great job he had done with a particular project.

Most of the time it just doesn't occur to the HMHP boss to take the time to chat with people, to get to know people, and to remember their names and their successes.

Make sure you communicate your success and your employees' success to your HMHP boss. Let your boss know when to recognize someone on your team. Remember, your accomplishments are your boss's accomplishments. Your success is your boss's success. Making your boss look good is always welcome. So the best thing you can do for a HMHP boss is communicate your wins, your successes, your accomplishments.

So use these eleven tips to help you work more successfully for a high-maintenance boss. Knowing how to work with your high-maintenance boss will be a lot less stressful and will make both of you more successful.

Tip #1:   Get down to business

Tip #2:   Don't take it personally

Tip #3:   Give your HMHP boss only essential details

Tip #4:   Figure out what your high-maintenance boss wants

Tip #5:   Always approach your HMHP boss with solutions

Tip #6:   Look for the best product, fastest way to implement, or latest technology for your recommended solution

Tip #7:   Establish a timeline and priority for projects and requests

Tip #8:   Don't surprise your high-maintenance boss

Tip #9:   Show loyalty for your HMHP boss

Tip #10: Make sure your HMHP boss knows your strengths

Tip #11: Communicate your successes and your wins

Moving Forward

Don't expect to keep up with high-maintenance bosses. You won't be able to. But when you know what they need, give it to them in the way they want it: succinctly, in order of importance, the benefits and results with only the relevant detail.

Learn how to communicate effectively with HMHP bosses and you'll grow and learn. Expect every time you talk with them they may have a new idea or a new direction, and it will be up to you to put it into perspective for them.

Give them the process, give them the timeline, give them the reality, give them the update, and communicate your successes, your wins, your accomplishments.

CHAPTER 10

High-Maintenance Employees as High-Level Executives

"When placed in command—take charge."
—Norman Schwarzkopf

This chapter covers:
- Positive and negative characteristics of a HMHP CEO
- Skills for managing communication with HMHP CEOs
- How to give your HMHP CEO feedback
- The benefits of implementing a 360-degree feedback program, growth plans, succession plans, and mentoring programs

Rick had been president and CEO of his 2,000-employee company for five years. The company had been through several reorganizations within the past few years and had hired four new senior people in the past three months. Rick decided that a leadership program would help unite his people and get them working better as a team.

His management group consisted of twenty-five senior and midlevel managers. Our first undertaking in the leadership program with this team involved communicating and team building. At the beginning of the session, we asked each manager to choose one person with whom they wanted to improve their communications. The group unanimously chose their CEO. The group as a whole expressed their disappointment that the president and CEO did not participate in our session. Rick is considered to be a high-maintenance CEO by those he works with. One of the most difficult challenges this group had was communicating with him. His attitude was that the program sounded great for fixing his team without his participation.

Because of the group's concern, we focused on the problems they were having in communicating with their CEO. The group identified these problems:

- The CEO's style was often geared towards crisis management.
- There was inconsistency in direction; orders were often changed.
- He set unrealistic deadlines for noncritical work with no discussion.
- The CEO most often used a messenger for communication with the team, leaving no opportunity for two-way communication.
- He micromanaged; the team felt there was a lack of respect for their time and their work.
- He had a lack of long-range and short-range vision, and an inability to make his vision meaningful to the group effort.
- He was too focused on the bottom line and not the process.
- Important details weren't always considered.

Many of the problems identified by the management team are characteristic of the HMHP CEO.

Like that of our high-maintenance employees, high-maintenance CEOs are driven people. They like to have control. Most of the time high-maintenance CEOs are moving very quickly. Their sense of drive and urgency propel the business but can also be difficult to work with. They thrive on positive change and are impatient by nature. This can be difficult especially for those people who are process oriented and analytical, like many of the senior and midlevel managers on Rick's team.

Room for Improvement

The management team was willing to work on their strategy for improving their communication with the CEO. In the next step, we developed a plan to communicate with this CEO.

- Be concise; be prepared.
- Present information with multiple forms and solutions; offer options that the team can live with.
- Always clarify expectations before leaving a meeting.
- Define obstacles of goals and consequences, and advise him on the current process of dealing with the problems and challenges.
- Give him feedback on the facts and identify the gaps that are getting in the way of a solution.
- Implement process improvement; for instance, tracking systems.
- Establish regular communication with him and send emails more regularly.
- Communicate via email and then copy to the person who's second in command, the senior vice president in this case.
- When facing a challenge, tell him: here are the challenges we face, here are a few options we have to overcome, which do you recommend?
- Identify his goals and expectations more clearly.
- To help build an environment of trust, have all of the senior VPs report directly to him.

Many of the solutions they came up with are the same as those recommended in the last chapter for working for any high-maintenance boss. But there was an even greater challenge for this group once they finished the list. Among all of the senior vice presidents and all the management team members, no one was willing to give this CEO feedback for fear of the effect it might have on their own jobs. They felt that the CEO would view them as not being loyal. They also felt they would be blind-siding him as they believed (and accurately so) that this CEO had no idea that his team felt this way.

Direct communication works best with the high-maintenance CEO or and high-maintenance employee. Often times they are moving so quickly they don't notice that others around them are frustrated. High-maintenance CEOs don't like to make mistakes. They tend to be hard on themselves and have a strong desire to succeed.

Providing Candid Feedback

Some of the options that they discussed in dealing with this CEO were to have someone he trusts, though not directly tied to the management team, give him feedback. A second option was to have senior management participate in a 360-degree feedback program, which is also sometimes referred to as a multirate tool.

The feedback is anonymously administered online. While you as the person receiving feedback may know that there are X number of peers giving you feedback, you won't know how each person in the rater group scored you on any one item. The report gives you an overall score in each category surveyed.

The term 360-degree feedback was coined with a compass in mind. It's a circle with 360 points of reference that determines and monitors a certain direction. The feedback received from a 360-degree feedback tool comes from all points of reference in the workplace. Those who participate in giving feedback should include individuals who work closely with the 360-degree recipient. That includes your boss, your colleagues, your direct reports, and yourself. This enables you to get a clear picture of how your skills and competencies are perceived by others and how you can maximize them to become more successful.

A 360-degree feedback report is valuable in a variety of areas, including personal development, to help employees master the skills needed in their present job or to prepare them for a new one; for team development, to stimulate high-performance teams to reach new heights, and also for change management.

The 360-degree feedback focuses on answering three basic questions:
• How can improving my performance help me in my career?
• How do I need to improve?
• How can I improve?

Using 360-degree feedback will help the HMHP CEOs see how they, too, can grow and develop, maximize their strengths, and explore areas for development.

Most companies hire an external vendor to process a 360-degree feedback assessment so it will stay completely confidential. It is time consuming to manually process responses, so most vendors now have online assessment tools that are simple and convenient for both receivers and senders of the feedback.

HMHP senior executives may find it challenging to process how others perceive them. So it is also important to work with a certified or professionally trained 360-degree feedback assessment coach, so that participants are able to review the feedback and ask questions about their individual results confidently and honestly. The HMHP executive will need to have a conversation about the feedback with the written report as supporting detail.

Here are important steps for a 360-degree feedback session to be a success and some things to avoid.

The 360-degree feedback report is an excellent tool for providing feedback anonymously. It is designed to create a foundation to maximize your strengths and to explore areas for individual development. With this tool, when people receive feedback from others, they not only get a detailed picture of how they see themselves, but how they are viewed by others, including their peers and their boss.

As I've discussed, high-maintenance employees have a difficult time receiving negative feedback. The 360-degree process helps them overcome this obstacle in two important ways. First, the feedback, which shows them the results, is in writing. Second, it shows them the path for improvement and sets goals for moving forward. It is particularly helpful for HMHP CEOs where their focus is on company results rather than personal growth and there is often the perception that there is no need for continuous personal growth.

What to avoid

There are some pitfalls to avoid when you choose to use a 360-degree program. Be aware that using a 360 feedback tool in the following ways can solicit feedback that is not honest and create a culture that is not open to giving performance feedback in positive ways. They include:

- Forcing the program on anyone
- Connecting it to any compensation decision
- Using the process at lower levels when it's not used by upper-level management

What you must do

On the other hand, it is important to introduce and execute a 360-degree program with these key steps to build trust and enhance the usefulness of the outcomes:

- Explain the process carefully before beginning.
- Align the process with the organization's culture, procedures, and practices.
- Provide structured follow-up and action plans.
- Keep all aspects confidential.
- Customize the feedback questions specifically to the needs of the job.
- Use certified, trained professionals.

It is particularly important to avoid using untrained professionals to facilitate the process. Trying to complete the process without certified, trained professionals often results in breaches of confidentiality by leaking or talking about a person's results, hammering recipients with the results after they have been shared with the facilitator, failing to facilitate action plans and follow-ups, or even threatening raters.

The importance of feedback to personal growth

When you receive any type of feedback, whether it's formal, informal, requested, or solicited, you can decide to use it to select changes or not. That may help develop whatever your full potential is. If you keep this in mind, it can be useful. The main purpose of most self-development efforts is to improve one's own effectiveness. Efforts to improve begin only after you learn and accept that your practices are ineffective.

Receiving clear, specific feedback from several reliable sources will help the HMHP CEO understand his or her true strengths and developmental needs better than with any other learning tool or method. Learning experiences that include feedback produce significantly more change than learning experiences without feedback. HMHP CEOs cannot meet every need of every person that they work with, but meeting the more critical needs of the majority of the people should be their goal in attempting to sustain or improve their effectiveness.

Developing a CEO Growth Plan

Without a commitment to improving upon the growth areas identified in the 360-degree feedback program, most likely, there will be no growth. HMHP high level executives who can see how the improvements tie into their success and the success of the company goals will commit to a growth plan.

As a CEO and company leader, I believe it is our job to unlock potential in others. Leadership is ultimately helping other people achieve more than they thought possible. We as leaders need to grow our own capabilities and in turn help those we lead to do the same.

For HMHP CEOs, it is important to lead by example. So it is particularly beneficial for high level executives to understand what is important for their own growth and development. What do they, as leaders, contribute? Under what conditions are they most likely to be successful? What are their blind spots? Under what conditions are they least likely to be successful?

A growth plan lists the competencies required for good leadership and provides questions that will help a high-maintenance CEO evaluate not only where he or she needs to build on existing strengths and weakness but also a way to continue the growth and development process. This is also a tool that helps an organization to build on the talents of its leaders and potential leaders. It is also an example of how to create a culture where performance feedback is given on an ongoing basis, not just at annual reviews. A sample template appears at the end of this chapter listing leadership competencies to help develop a growth plan for the HMHP CEO. But remember that while many have tried to create a definitive list of leadership competencies, there is no one ultimate source and you should tailor yours to your situation.

When a well-run 360-degree feedback program starts with upper-level management and then is used with mid- and first-level managers, it may identify some people who are high-maintenance employees who are true leaders, who can grow and become part of your senior executive team. Succession planning and mentoring can provide opportunities to develop the HMHP wealth in your company. That process starts with the CEO.

Temporary Support Systems

Once the change effort is complete, the last step is to assess and dismantle the temporary support systems that are no longer required. You may find that some of these support systems may actually serve a continued, useful purpose and may incorporate them as a formal part of your new state.

Communicating the Company's Vision

As stated throughout this book, communication is the primary role of leaders and the most important skill for high-level executives. Many high-maintenance CEOs and other high-level executives tend to keep a lot in their heads and sometimes that includes the vision they have for the company. It is important that they communicate the company's vision and do so often.

Just as it is important for other HMHP managers to create opportunities to talk with their staff members, this behavior is also important for HMHP high-level executives. High-maintenance employees need to talk one-on-one with their potential leaders on a regular basis. They need to encourage two-way communication by asking for opinions. When talking, they should do less telling and ask questions before giving answers.

Using programs such as 360-degree feedback, growth and succession planning, and mentoring will help the HMHP CEO create an environment of trust, one that opens the door for better communication and growth for high-maintenance employees as well as others.

Moving Forward

Having a high-maintenance CEO can present challenges to other senior executives. It is imperative for both sides in this relationship to learn how to leverage the strengths of such an individual while also helping him or her to grow and overcome weaknesses that might inhibit organizational success.

The high-maintenance CEO must recognize the need to constantly communicate the vision, manage change in a carefully planned way, set clear and realistic goals and performance expectations, and give appropriate feedback to help others improve their performance. Another key part of the CEO's role is to establish a personal growth plan, a succession plan, and a mentoring program to developing the next round of leaders.

Those who report to a high-maintenance CEO need to be willing to give the boss honest feedback when he or she is failing to communicate in a way that is productive for the executive team or others in the organization. Valuable tools such as a 360-degree feedback program can make this feedback process less risky and more productive for all involved.

High-maintenance CEOs can succeed best when they master communicating with people at all levels of the organization. While this is a challenge for many high-maintenance performers, it is one that must be met if the company is to more forward toward its vision.

Leadership Growth Plan

Score your leadership/management competencies on the chart to the right. For each competency, put a check mark in the box that best describes how you meet the organization's standards.

Based on your ratings, identify areas for improvement by answering the following questions.

- What are your three strengths?
- What are your three areas for development?
- What are your blind spots as leaders?
- How do they prevent you from sometimes getting what you want?
- Who do you seek feedback from to improve your own performance?

Name:			
Skills	Exceeds Standards	At Standards	Below Standard
Leadership/ Management Competencies			
Conflict and Problem Resolution			
Getting Results			
Leadership Focus			
Opportunity Analysis			
Planning Orientation			
Goal Orientation			
Self and Project Management			
Staffing Focus			
Empathetic Outlook			
Emotional Control			
Proactive Thinking			
Results Orientation			
Accountability for Others			
Developing Others			
Evaluating Others			
Monitoring Others			
Practical Thinking			
Attention to Detail			
Consistency and Reliability			
Quality Orientation			
Personal Commitment			
Self-Direction			
Self-Discipline			
Other:			
Other:			

AFTERWORD

If by reading this book you have discovered you are a HMHP, my hope is that you will embrace these three ideas to move you along a path of success:

- Understand the strengths and weaknesses of your own behavior so that, to be successful, you can adapt your communication style when necessary.
- Working with others who have different behavioral styles can be of great benefit to you if you know how to use their strengths to complement your weaknesses.
- Finding the right job or role for you within your organization can change your outlook from frustrated to satisfied, self-motivated, and happy.

For those who find themselves working for or surrounded by high-maintenance employees, my hope is you will learn to put them in a position to use their strengths and help them compensate for their weaknesses:

- These are the next generation leaders; cultivate them in order for your business to succeed and grow.
- Coach and lead them so they learn about the behaviors they need to exhibit in the workplace in order to be successful and realize their full potential.

- Reward and work to retain them by keeping them challenged and feeling the importance of their contributions to the overall success of the company.

Most of all, it is important to spend time with your high-maintenance employees. Being open to different approaches in order to communicate, coach, and lead them is important to keeping them on the right track. If you can't do it, have them work with someone who can, but keep your high-maintenance employees challenged; help them be happy in their job.

INDEX

D

E

F

U

About the Author

For over twenty years, Katherine Graham Leviss, president of XBCoaching, has been showing companies how to improve results and grow their businesses. Through testing, training, and business coaching, Katherine has helped thousands of chief executives, front-line managers, and sales groups develop employees into organizationally-minded problem solvers, create highly productive work teams, integrate cross-cultural workforces, start new departments, and more.

Her fast climb up several corporate ladders as account executive, sales manager, co-owner, and managing director have given her a depth and breadth of business experience to share. Her client list spans thirty-eight states and a broad range of industries, including, but by no means limited to:

- Broadcast Industry
- Pharmaceutical Industry
- Retail
- Financial Industry
- Telecommunications Industry
- Education
- Health Care
- Upscale Home Construction

- Sports
- Gas and Energy
- Hospitality

In addition to writing her own quarterly e-zine with advice for managing and running a business, she has published articles such as "Hiring Department Managers That Are a Perfect Fit" and "How to Successfully Incorporate a New Member into Your Team" in other e-zines and on sites across the World Wide Web.

Katherine is a certified executive coach through Corporate Coach University. She is a certified behavioral analyst and a certified values analyst as well as a certified attribute index analyst. Her rigorous training for these certification programs qualifies Katherine as an expert in understanding personal behaviors and values that provide the basis for her understanding of different behavioral attributes and methodologies for dealing with these attributes in the workplace. Katherine received her BA in Communications from Boston University. She is a member of the International Coaching Federation and The American Society of Training and Development.